ARE GAY RIGHTS RIGHT?

ЭАМОН

ARE GAY RIGHTS RIGHT?

Updated Edition

Making Sense of the Controversy

Roger J. Magnuson

MULTNOMAH

Portland, OR 97266

Unless otherwise indicated, all Scripture references are from the King James Version.

ARE GAY RIGHTS RIGHT?
© 1990 The Berean League Fund
Published by Multnomah Press
Portland, Oregon 97266

Cover design by Durand Demlow.

Printed in the United States of America.

Library of Congress Cataloging-in-Publication Data

Magnuson, Roger J., 1945-
    Are gay rights right? : making sense of the controversy / Roger J. Magnuson.
        p. cm.
    Includes bibliographical references.
    ISBN 0-88070-336-9
    1. Gay liberation movement—United States. 2. Homosexuality—Religious aspects. 3. Sodomy—United States. 4. Homosexuality—Law and legislation—United States. I. Title.
HQ76.8.U5M34 1990
305.90664—dc20   89-48819
                                             CIP

92 93 94 95 96 97 98 99 - 10 9 8 7 6 5 4 3 2

Those who indulge in perversion tell those who are living normal lives that it is they who are deviating from what is natural. They think they are following a natural life themselves. They are like people on a ship who think it is those on shore who are moving away. Language is relative everywhere. But we need a fixed point by which to judge it. So the harbor is that fixed point for those who are moving aboard ship. But in morality, where are we going to find a harbor?

Blaise Pascal

Contents

Introduction

The best lack all conviction, while the worst
Are full of passionate intensity.
"The Second Coming"
W. B. Yeats

The difference in intensity between the best and the worst is nowhere confirmed more graphically than in the growing power of homosexual rights organizations in America. Their intensity and surprising successes cause many to wonder whether Yeats's pessimism is justified: "Things fall apart, the center cannot hold."

The obstacles these groups have faced, and to some degree surmounted, are formidable:

Laws in many states making consensual sodomy criminal.

The natural revulsion normal people feel in the face of sexual perversion—a reaction homosexuals refer to as "homophobia."

The documented history of wild promiscuity suggesting that the average male homosexual has had over five hundred different partners.

Enormous public health costs caused directly and proximately by homosexual conduct (homosexuals, though perhaps fewer than 5 percent of the population, carry a majority of the nation's syphilis).

A major role in the AIDS epidemic, which according to the *Wall Street Journal* will cost the economy over sixty billion dollars in the next year.

A historic timidity about revealing perverse sexual practices to family and friends, what homosexuals call "coming out."

Notwithstanding these barbed thickets of common perceptions and common sense, homosexuals in the last decade have been bringing demands, sometimes quite successfully, on several fronts. These demands have one objective. As Dennis Altman writes in *The Homosexualization of America*, "The emergence of the modern gay movement [was] characterized by a willingness to demand not just tolerance but *total acceptance* and by a new militance in making these demands" (emphasis added).

The strategic vision of "total acceptance" articulated by homosexuals such as Altman and others means public legitimacy, credibility, and community endorsement: in short, making sexual deviance as acceptable as sexual normalcy.

To accomplish that objective, homosexuals now fight tactical battles on three fronts:

1. Where homosexuality is prohibited by law, as in the case of laws prohibiting sodomy, homosexuals seek to repeal those laws or have them declared unconstitutional by the courts.

2. Where there are practices permitted by the law to heterosexuals but not to homosexuals

(for example, marriage or adoption of children), homosexuals seek equivalent privileges for themselves.

3. Where the personal discretion or decision making of individuals impinges on homosexuals—a landlord's choice not to rent practicing homosexuals a room, for example—homosexuals seek to pass laws that actually create special privileges for homosexual behavior ("gay rights laws") that are not available for people with more normal behavior.

Society can take one of three approaches with immoral or socially irresponsible behavior. It can prohibit it (a law against sodomy); it can tolerate it (repeal the law against sodomy or simply not enforce it); it can prefer it (by giving special privileges to those who practice it). It is the third stage which homosexuals seek to attain in contemporary society.

GAY ADVANCES

The homosexual rights movement has experienced some surprising successes:

• Compelling Georgetown University, a Roman Catholic institution, to accept and provide facilities for homosexual organizations on campus contrary to its long-standing and sincerely held moral teachings.

• Organizing a homosexual public high school in New York City, at taxpayers' expense, and staging a popular play for high school students that depicts efforts of a wealthy Malibu show business personality to find the prettiest boy in the school. Finding him, he brings him back to his California hideaway to do perverted acts on a waterbed filled with Dom Perignon.

• Controlling many state-run educational efforts on AIDS and using public dollars to print brochures and other materials encouraging elementary school students to think of perverted acts as normal; to hold "condom awareness" classes for adolescents; and to urge juveniles to consider experimentation with homosexual acts.

• Convincing a majority of public health officials throughout the country to treat AIDS differently from any other past epidemic by permitting anonymous testing and by refusing to enforce provisions of various state laws which require tracing of all sexual contacts.

• Intimidating members of the American Psychiatric Association, through a variety of disruptive tactics, to remove homosexuality from the list of mental disorders. A later confidential poll revealed a majority of psychiatrists continued to think that homosexuality was a "pathological" condition.

• Spinning the facts of the AIDS epidemic so ingeniously that many blame the government for not working hard enough to come up with a cure, rather than blaming those who knowingly practice behavior that exposes them to the disease. The result is an enormous research effort on AIDS that has siphoned money from research on diseases that people cannot avoid by simply changing their behavior, such as cancer, Alzheimer's, arthritis, and multiple sclerosis.

• Convincing mayors in a half dozen of the nation's largest cities to participate in "gay pride" days to celebrate sexually deviant behavior.

WHAT DOES THE FUTURE HOLD?

As surprising as these successes have been, the lingering question is what do they mean for the future? We can measure the huge transformation in American values over the last two decades and see how a prominent homosexual social commentator can describe it as the "homosexualization" of America. But social forces, once set in motion, operate by a Newtonian law of inertia. Once in motion they stay in motion unless they meet some superior force. If we extrapolate from the last two decades, we must ask where we will be two decades from now. If the breathtaking pace of acceptance of perverted sexual behavior continues, the world of the early twenty-first century will hardly be imaginable from the perspective of today.

Already the dim outlines of that future are being sketched by those on the cutting edge of homosexual ideology. Coming into view is the homosexual vision of a world where all sexual activity is placed beyond the rule of moral norms. The final destination for this ideology is a city of polymorphous and perverse sexuality where anything goes.

The final expression of this view will come in the push to legalize sex with children. It is already talked about by members of the homosexual community. It has long been an objective of many militant members of the homosexual movement. What appears shocking to us today may not be so shocking tomorrow.

The North American Man/Boy Love Association (NAMBLA) is carrying the ideology of the homosexual movement to its natural conclusion. If there is no such thing as perversion and if sex is good, the exercise of the merely physical appetite, then why should children be denied this good?

NAMBLA takes the view that sex is good, that homosexuality is good not only for adults, but for young people as well. We support all consensual sexual relationships regardless of age. As long as the relationship is mutually pleasurable and no one's rights are violated, sex should be no one else's business.[1]

Or as NAMBLA puts it again:

Sexual liberation cannot be achieved without the liberation of children. This means many things. Children need to gain control over their lives, a control which they are denied on all sides. They need to break the yoke of "protection" which alienates them from themselves, a "protection" imposed on them by adults—their family, the schools, the state, and prevailing sexual and social mores.[2]

So much for the ideology. The concrete proposals will surely follow. Again, NAMBLA has an idea:

There is no age at which a person becomes capable of consenting to sex. The age of sexual consent is just one of many ways in which adults impose their system of control on children. . . . The state is the enemy of freedom, not its guarantor. The best evidence against the argument that children cannot consent to sex, including with adults, is the fact that millions do it anyway.[3]

The force of the movement continues in motion. First it is necessary to break down societal prohibitions against immoral behavior. Next it is important to establish social tolerance of that behavior. Finally, there will be efforts to make that behavior the preferred behavior.

Faced with these developments, the average citizen sometimes feels like a pedestrian attempting to stop a roaring locomotive. The opposition attempts to create a sense of historical inevitability about these social changes. Some politicians are inordinately influenced by a small but determined minority of homosexual militants. The media give out megadoses of propaganda that define the issues in a way most favorable to the homosexual agenda. A great iron triangle of a special-interest group (the homosexual lobby), the media (filled with issues consultants), and compliant legislators insures that programs are sensitive to homosexuals. The locomotive rolls on and liberationist rhetoric forms a formidable cowcatcher that flips out of the way any isolated moral or political opposition.

REASONS FOR OPTIMISM

Those feelings of loneliness and isolation are not, however, necessary nor is ultimate defeat self-evident. The last decade has shown that groups of citizens can effectively fight this onslaught of homosexual activism. There is no need for negativism. As important as what the homosexuals have done is what they have not done. Among other things, homosexuals have not been able to

• *Convince Congress to enact civil rights protections for homosexuals equivalent to those provided for racial and other minorities.* Despite the routine introduction of bills attempting to create civil rights protection for homosexuals, spanning over ten years, homosexuals have never been successful in getting those bills out of committee, even with a liberal Congress eager to pass civil rights measures.

• *Convince the Supreme Court that there is a constitutional right to practice consensual sodomy.* To the contrary, the Supreme Court has now held that there is no right to commit homosexual sodomy under the Constitution, and that it is perfectly acceptable to criminalize acts of sodomy between consenting adults.

• *Convince any state legislatures, except two (Wisconsin and Massachusetts), to have state-wide civil rights protection for homosexuals.* Notwithstanding heavily organized homosexual efforts to get states to pass civil rights protection for homosexuals, only two have been successful.

• *Convince most Americans that homosexual behavior is normal and ought to be given special protections.* On nearly every occasion when homosexual rights measures have been put to the voters, they have been resoundingly defeated. Beginning with Dade County, Florida, in 1978 and continuing with the resounding rebuke to a popular governor in an Oregon referendum in 1988 and surprising defeats to homosexual legislation in referendums in Irvine, California, and even San Francisco itself in 1989, the voters speak clearly, often overwhelmingly, on this issue.

Four recent examples show the possibilities for action. In Mankato, Minnesota, a routine press story in the local newspaper alerted a few citizens that the local city council was preparing to adopt a gay rights measure. One moving force behind the measure was a popular professor at Mankato State University. A quick head count of the city council made it clear that they favored the measure. But despite their lack of political experience, an organized group of concerned citizens went to work. They distributed literature to the city council. They had a rally to present evidence on the issue and to mobilize their supporters. They called the city council repeatedly, quietly but firmly arguing for rejection of the measure. They prayed and worked and got on the radio talk shows. The result? The city council flip-flopped. Not only did the council reject the measure, but one of the sponsors changed her mind and voted against it.

In Pittsburgh, a gay rights measure looked like a *fait accompli*. The local gay rights lobby had talked with the city council members, and there were enough votes to pass it based on the declared feelings of the city council. A local Christian-oriented television station got involved, as did several ministers, spanning the theological spectrum. They brought in speakers. They passed out literature. Notwithstanding the apparent hopelessness of the task, they decided to use their best efforts to fight the measure. To their surprise, the city council, with several members reversing themselves, voted the proposal down.

In Oregon, a popular new governor came down with an executive order barring "discrimination" against homosexuals in state government. The maneuver cleverly avoided the political pitfalls experienced by homosexual measures elsewhere. It required no legislative approval; it was simply done. A number of people opposing the measure found a way to bring it to the voters by initiative. The initial polls showed the governor's measure, apparently so fair-sounding, was well ahead—in some early polls by over twenty points. The political analysts gave the initiative scant hope of success. But when the votes were counted, the proponents of the initiative won a remarkable victory. The governor's action was rescinded.

In San Francisco, the city government passed a "domestic partners" law that gave to homosexual partners certain privileges previously limited to married couples. Some local ministers mounted what many viewed as a hopelessly quixotic referendum campaign against the law. Given the sizable homosexual population in the city and its long-time reputation for laissez-faire morality and a storied tolerance for eccentric life-styles, some analysts suggested that a 40 percent vote for the referendum would be a setback for the homosexual community. But when the votes were counted, the referendum won by a clear majority and the domestic partners law was repealed—in the most homosexually oriented city in the world.

THE CRITICAL ROLE OF EDUCATION

What made the difference in these successful campaigns? There are many reasons, both strategic and tactical. But one factor is preeminent: education. Facts become the ammunition. There is no substitute in any political debate for the intelligent deployment of demonstrable facts. Facts have an impact. Facts work changes. It is typical in these political struggles for gay rights proposals to ignite quickly and become popular with both city council members and the public. It is popular to be against "discrimination" and for the provision of "civil rights." Knees jerk predictably when the right political stimulus is given. Good people want to be fair. They do not want to deny anyone, least of all a minority, any rights they might otherwise have. Early polls reflect this bias.

But when citizens educate themselves, and then the general public, the polls change. Minds change.

Once the slogans are put aside and the real meaning of gay rights is dispassionately analyzed, gay rights militants are usually put to flight.

The key element, therefore, is to know the facts. Most people opposed to gay rights first react with a visceral revulsion. Homosexuals call this distaste homophobia, but it is only the natural revulsion a normal person feels in the face of sexual perversion. Many others react with a moral objection: homosexual behavior is not right. Or they advance a religious argument: the Bible says homosexuality is wrong. A majority which does not acknowledge the validity of these arguments is often unmoved, and the arguments are easily stigmatized as a moralistic intrusion into the political process. To fight successfully against gay rights proposals, citizens must arm themselves with facts that serve as objective confirmation of their moral reservations about homosexual behavior.

The purpose of this book is to demonstrate that such facts are abundant. Those interested in sound public policy will find overwhelming arguments against giving special privileges to homosexual behavior. The arguments are legal, medical, sociological, economic, and psychological. They are based on facts that belie the slogans and images of homosexual ideology. For those seriously interested in the commonweal, it is necessary to fortify the mind with an armamentarium of information. Ideas have consequences. Knowledge is power. Truth liberates. The remaining chapters of this book set out the arguments against gay rights.

Introduction, Notes

1. Enrique Rueda and Michael Schwartz, *Gays, Aids and You* (Greenwich, Conn.: Devin-Adair Publishers, 1987), 67.
2. Ibid., 68.
3. Ibid., 69.

Chapter One

Defining the Issues:
The Power of Language

> *In our time, it is broadly true that political writing is bad writing. . . . Political speech and writing are largely the defense of the indefensible. . . . Thus political language has to consist largely of euphemism, question-begging and sheer cloudy vagueness.*
>
> George Orwell

*I*rving Bieber was a distinguished scholar. He was the primary author of a 1962 book titled *Homosexuality*. One of the foremost psychoanalysts of this century, Bieber had long known that "all psychoanalytic theories assume that homosexuality is psychopathologic."[1]

It was now May 1970 and Bieber had been invited to address the annual meeting of the American Psychiatric Association. Bieber was to appear on a panel addressing the issues of homosexuality and the transsexual. Bieber was of course familiar with the robust debate that characterized serious psychoanalytic discussion. He knew words were the primary weapons of academic psychiatric warfare. But he was not ready for the kind of weaponry that would be directed his way on this occasion.

A loosely organized confederation of homosexuals and feminists were preparing to confront him in a way that reflected disdain for the traditional rules of language and logic in Bieber's scholarly profession. Influenced by the radicalization of American politics in 1970, a year that saw the high-water mark of protest, they decided to welcome him with tactics that observers would call "guerrilla theater."[2] As Bieber began to speak, he was immediately the object of shouted taunts from the audience. His voice was drowned out by chants. When he attempted to explain his position, the militants laughed in derision. For Bieber that day there would be no civility, only expressions of rage, calumny, and vicious personal attack. No wonder one observer described Bieber as in "considerable distress."[3]

In a later session on sexuality, the "guerrillas" again came out in force. A young Australian doctor who had successfully used conditioning techniques in the treatment of perverse sexual practices attempted to read his paper. The visitors in the scholarly audience were not prepared to listen. "Where did you take your residency—Auschwitz?" After using words such as "vicious" and "torture," the demonstrators demanded to take the microphone. The result was pandemonium. Homosexual militants shouted out their outrage and described psychiatry as an instrument of oppression.[4]

Bieber had seen only the vanguard of the homosexual shock troops. Disruptions continued. At the frequently somnolent Convocation of Fellows of the A.P.A., homosexual activists stormed the meeting, grabbed the microphone, and denounced the psychiatrists, seeking to intimidate them from even discussing homosexuality. As one homosexual leader declared, "Psychiatry is the enemy incarnate. Psychiatry has waged a relentless war of extermination against us. You may take this as a declaration of war against you." Some of the psychiatrists viewed the homosexual militants as nothing more than "Nazi storm troopers." The psychiatric profession had never before seen forged credentials, physical intimidation, and brutal rhetoric used at a scholarly meeting.[5]

The object of the homosexuals' fury was, of course, a long-held tenet of the psychiatric profession: homosexuality, based on a wealth of evidence, is a pathological condition, not a normal outlet of sexual expression. Homosexuality had long been listed in the *Diagnostic and Statistical Manual, Mental Disorders (DSM-I)*. It was, therefore, a "mental disorder." As Dr. Karl Menninger had written several years earlier, "Whatever it be called by the public, there is no question in the minds of psychiatrists regarding the abnormality of such behavior."[6]

It would have been difficult for Bieber to believe that such brutal, unsophisticated, and unscholarly assaults could change the results of scholarly research. But the homosexual objective was clear. They wanted homosexuality deleted from *DSM-II*. And, shockingly, the homosexual militants won. In what some viewed as a "craven capitulation to the power of the mob,"[7] the A.P.A. decided to delete homosexuality from its list of mental disorders.

Many dissenters were outraged. The profession had "disgraced itself." Another observer said, "It now seems that if groups of people march and raise enough hell, they can change anything in time . . . will schizophrenia be next?"[8] And one psychiatrist wrote: "The board of trustees has made a terrible, almost unforgivable decision which will adversely affect the lives of young homosexuals who are desperately seeking direction and cure. That decision . . . will give [them] an easy way out."[9] Among the most sensible voices was senior psychiatrist Abram Kardiner who wrote:

> Those who reinforce the disintegrative elements in our society will get no thanks from future generations. The family becomes the ultimate victim of homosexuality, a result which any society can tolerate only within certain limits.

> If the American Psychiatric Association endorses one of the symptoms of social distress as a normal phenomenon, it demonstrates to the public its ignorance . . . and thereby acquires a responsibility for aggravating the already-existing chaos.[10]

A new rhetoric had won the day. But had it really changed the minds of psychiatrists? A revealing, confidential poll later showed that the earlier decision was the product of intimidation. A poll in the journal *Medical Aspects of Human Sexuality*, taken three years after the A.P.A.'s 1974 referendum, sought the views of ten thousand psychiatrists on whether homosexuality was pathological. One analysis of the first responses to the poll revealed that 69 percent continued to believe that homosexuality "usually represented a pathological adaptation." Only 18 percent disagreed with this proposition. When asked the source of homosexual problems, 70 percent said it was the result of "personal conflicts" rather than social stigmatization.[11]

A tainted victory won by a savage use of verbal weapons became a chief arguing point for homosexuals. Homosexuals now could use the edict of a major academic organization to declare their normalcy.

THE POWER OF LANGUAGE

The political success with Professor Bieber's colleagues was born of a new militancy among homosexuals who understood the power of language. In his "Politics and the English Language,"[12] George Orwell showed that language is not a servile handmaiden of political debate. Indeed, it often calls the shots. Language shapes, defines, motivates, and in large measure determines the answer in political debate by the way it states the question. To think clearly on an issue, one must precisely define it. In this arena as in all others, Orwell pointed out, clear thinking requires clear language. The "slovenliness of our language," he said, "makes it easier for us to have foolish thoughts." If "one gets rid of these habits, one can think more clearly, and to think clearly is a necessary first step to political regeneration."

Political pollsters have long known this relationship. Most people do not favor "abortion on demand." On the other hand, most people are against taking away a woman's "constitutional right" to "control her own body" or to "terminate a pregnancy." Curiously, many people can be lured into contradictory positions simply by the pollster's choice of words. They are for "reproductive freedom" and for the "rights of unborn children." Few people want, in their heart of hearts, to be either "anti-choice" or "anti-life."

Words used in political debate frequently carry

heavy emotional baggage. It is virtually impossible for anyone to rise up against offering any group of people their rights. It is equally impossible to be in favor of discrimination. Rights are as American as Thomas Paine; discrimination is a black person trudging silently to the back of the bus. Yet such terms more often confuse than illuminate political issues. There are rights whose creation nearly everyone agrees would threaten the continued existence of society: the right to steal, to mug, to refuse to pay taxes. There are forms of discrimination that serve as the foundation of a just system of law. Indeed, why is a person of good judgment called "discriminating"? Every person, no matter what his role, must exercise wise discretion in life, and discretion presupposes a range of available options from which one tries to choose the best or avoid the worst. The judge, in his discretion, must determine whether the plaintiff or the defendant has the better claims and treat him accordingly. The employer, in his discretion, must determine who among his employees is the most diligent and who deserves a raise in pay or quick advancement. The wise shopper discriminates in the choice of products at the supermarket. As one observer has put it:

> Each distinction we erase makes it harder for us to see or make other distinctions. The ability to discriminate is, of course, essential to the ability to choose. If we lose it, the change in our own character cannot help but profoundly change the character of our government. And what sort of government do you suppose it would be?[13]

During the last decade, a new group has formed to demand its rights and to put an end to discrimination.

The controversy has grown out of a radically new political movement in America, summed up in the slogan "Gay Rights" and dating its formal beginning to June 1969, from a riot at the Stonewall Bar in Greenwich Village in New York City. Before that incident, homosexual political activism had made only fleeting trips out of the closet in American political life. In 1948, there was a "Bachelors for Wallace" group that spoke of organizing those with "our physiological and psychological handicaps . . . toward the constructive social progress of mankind."[14] Homosexuals frequently viewed themselves as handicapped prior to the new ideology:

> Many of us homosexuals regard our inversion as a handicap because it precludes a complete life. And no life is complete emotionally or biologically without the extension of love and the upbringing of children of one's own . . . to boast of being glad for an exclusively homosexual condition is but a defense mechanism.[15]

The 1950s and 1960s saw the appearance of groups such as the Mattachine Society (for male homosexuals) and the Daughters of Bilitis (for lesbians) that edged their way tentatively into the American political scene.[16] In 1961, there was a stir when the first homosexual political candidate, Jose Sarria, ran for city supervisor in San Francisco.[17] But none of these efforts generated significant momentum for the movement, or even widespread attention, until the Stonewall riot.

THE STONEWALL RIOT

It started out as a routine police raid on a bar known for illegal sexual behavior. The police arrived, saw what they expected, and began making arrests. But instead of surrendering to the police, the patrons fought back with bricks and stones and epithets. The radicalization of America in the late 1960s, with the Yippies, the Weathermen, the Black Panthers, and a host of other groups riding the crest of the anti-war movement, had percolated its way through the homosexual community as well.

The Stonewall resistance was the spark that ignited an explosion of homosexual activism. Homosexuals began to urge that homosexuality not only be tolerated but also accepted as "good, right, and desirable for those who choose to engage in it."[18] The date of the Stonewall riot became "Gay Pride" day, celebrated throughout the United States, often with the blessing of local city councils.

The older homosexual organizations became "Uncle Toms." The new militants became "the children of Christopher Street," and "gay liberation" forces began to link their political agenda to other efforts of rebellion against an allegedly repressive society.

A year later, homosexuals staged an anniversary of the Stonewall riot, demanding the repeal of sodomy laws and mobilizing previously closeted homosexuals into a public demonstration. Homosexuals began verbal assaults against everything from the church to the mass media. Their "book burning" efforts resulted in the successful removal of books not sympathetic to their cause from many university libraries.[19] Homosexuals were on the march.

The most lasting result of the Stonewall riot was thus not a day but a movement. Its goal was, and is, total acceptance of homosexuality. In seeking that end, the movement ran up against two significant social impediments: laws that made homosexual conduct illegal (e.g., laws against sodomy) and language that made homosexual conduct unattractive (e.g., "sodomy"). A movement aggressively seeking full social acceptance had to clear both hurdles. Laws could be changed only if public perception were changed; public perception could be changed only if language were changed.

The gay rights controversy shows the mystifying power of language to forge a consensus. The homosexuals' use of clever expressions to convey a hidden meaning has been well explored by various writers. To be "compassionate" means to accept homosexual behavior. "A stable, loving relationship" means that homosexual pairings are equivalent to marriage. "Stereotyping" means it is irrational to assume that all homosexual practices are wrong. "Sexual minority" suggests that homosexuals are a legitimate minority. All such expressions are designed to put non-homosexuals on the defensive.

The language of such laws is simple on its face. Most gay rights ordinances forbid "discrimination" in housing, employment, and public accommodations based on a person's "affectional or sexual preference" or "affectional or sexual orientation."[20] They seek, in short, "gay rights."

While the words make fine political slogans, they do not advance clear political analysis. To accomplish that objective, it is necessary to define both the group seeking protection and the protection that group desires.

THE GROUP DEFINED: UNDERSTANDING THE TERMS *GAYS*, *AFFECTIONAL PREFERENCE*, AND *SEXUAL ORIENTATION*

Most male homosexuals call themselves *gays*. Female homosexuals frequently refer to themselves as *lesbians*, based on the alleged sexual practices of women on the isle of Lesbos.

Although nomenclature changes somewhat from place to place, the conventional formula is "gay men and lesbian women." *Gay* is used to suggest a cheerful, free, and sunny approach to life. *Lesbian* suggests something more assertive and masculine. Both project a consciously chosen identity, putting a more positive face on the respective groups than the taunting language of the street. Neither deals honestly with the underlying sexual behavior.

The same intent is behind the use of the terms *affectional preference* or *sexual orientation*. To be affectionate is an unqualified good, as warm and comfortable as a good lap dog. We like to receive and to give affection. To interrupt the affection two people have for one another comes off as a Scrooge-like interference in wholesome and humane relationships. The same is true of preferences. In a tolerant society, a gentleman always recognizes another's preferences. "Coffee—cream or sugar?" "Do you take tea with lemon, sir?" "Do you prefer it a little cooler?" asks the bellhop. Sexual orientation, on the other hand, suggests a predisposition or inclination that is both neutral and natural.

To see how language prejudges the issue, we need merely substitute some synonyms. Take, for example, the English equivalent. In England, what homosexuals do together is called *buggery*, both in law and on the street. Imagine a group calling for "buggers' rights" or speaking of "buggers' pride." The American equivalent in legal language is *sodomy*, defined generally as unnatural sexual relations, especially between male persons or between a human being and an animal. Imagine, if you will, a call for "sodomites' rights." To understand who is seeking protection, it is important to look beyond the terms *gay* and *affectional preference*, beyond images of men strolling together along the seashore of Greek islands thinking great thoughts and displaying tender affection—in short, beyond the language to get to an understanding of the group seeking protection.

Put plainly, gay rights laws are meant to protect men and women who practice oral and anal copulation with members of the same sex. In about half the states, their behavior violates criminal laws. In a televised debate, a questioner asked the head of a local human rights agency whether she thought there was really no moral difference between giving special protection to people of good character who happened to have been born black and giving special protection to men who made a voluntary choice to commit sodomy with other men. "Why," she blurted out, "gays would never do that."[21] Such is the power of language.

The test, then, is one of behavior, not status. Homosexuals can be characterized by what they do (sodomy) and with whom they do it (their own sex). What gay rights laws ask for is a special privilege for homosexuals not generally available to other groups, such as those who commit incest, adultery, bestiality, pedophilia or, for that matter, any other criminal or antisocial behavior.

THE RELIEF DESIRED: THE CREATION OF RIGHTS

The new gay rights laws offer homosexuals a special protection described as "rights." Gays should have basic rights, the argument runs, and some of these rights have been abridged. One may disagree with a person's preferences, after all, without denying him his rights.

Such language, of course, begs the question. If homosexuals really have the rights they claim, then they should not be abridged. A right is a moral and legal entitlement. It is the making of a claim that society must rightfully acknowledge. But two facts are often lost in the debate:

First, *homosexuals have rights already.* Homosexuals have legal rights identical to those of any other citizen. They may exercise their rights to free speech, to assemble, to exercise any religious preference, to be safe in their houses from unreasonable searches, to confront their accusers, to demand a jury trial in a civil or criminal proceeding. They may own property, travel abroad, buy and sell, and enter into enforceable contracts. They are armed with the same kinds of rights other Americans cherish.

Second, *all rights have corresponding duties.* Every newly created right gives rise to a corresponding duty in others. If a homosexual has the right to teach sex education courses in a public school, the school has a duty to allow him to do so, and the parent of a child in that school loses his right to have a say in the moral caliber of a person who teaches his child. If a homosexual has a right to rent a room in a rooming house owned by Mrs. Murphy, Mrs. Murphy loses her right to control the moral caliber of people who live in her house. Compare the following, admittedly fanciful, extremes:

A poor law student approaches Mrs. Murphy's door to see about the twenty-five-dollar-per-week room he had read about in the classified ads. Mrs. Murphy eyes him warily. She asks a series of questions, concluding with, "Do you like the music of J.S. Bach?" "Yes," he answers, somewhat confused. "Then you'll never rent a room from me!" she says and slams the door. What are the student's rights?

Two homosexuals, from an outlandish extreme of the movement, approach Mrs. Murphy's door, one in lipstick and wobbly high heels, the other dressed in leather and jeans, wearing a menacing chain around his neck. They inquire about the room. Mrs. Murphy, annoyed at their appearance and their distasteful, overtly sexual behavior, yells "No, thank you!" through a crack in the door and runs back into her rooming house. What are their "rights"?

Before the passage of a gay rights law, both the student and the homosexuals have the same rights: none. Mrs. Murphy's dislike for Bach may have been opinionated, ignorant, or confused. But the student has no right to claim special protection of the law for any of his personal preferences, whether they be a preference for Bach, cats, or peanut butter. Mrs. Murphy may not like his looks, his children, or his automobile. His only choice is to stop at the next advertised apartment on his want-ads checklist.

Before a gay rights law, situation number two comes out the same way. Here Mrs. Murphy seems on more solid ground. Her decision is based not on a whim but on her perception of the potential tenants' characters. Nonetheless, after passage of such a law, the homosexuals win a privilege for their unnatural sexual practices that the student does not have for his baroque musical tastes, or the average citizen for his normal preferences. The homosexuals can sue . . . and win.[22]

Laws that protect sexual preferences create a new and privileged class. From all the now-unprotected preferences there are in the world—for clothes, cars, gourmet food, pets, music, poetry—the gay rights laws carve out a special set of preferences related to perverted sexual behavior and give it a special protection available to no one else.[23]

The controversy boils down to this: Should special legal privileges not available to other Americans be created for homosexuals? And if so, should we be ready to confer similar privileges upon groups that practice other immoral, socially objectionable, or even illegal behavior? If the gay rights laws sail easily through city council chambers, a quick line could form at the door.

The next two chapters analyze more closely the nature of the group seeking these special privileges (chapter 2) and the legal ramifications of giving them what they seek (chapter 3).

Chapter 1, Notes

1. Irving Bieber et al., *Homosexuality: A Psychoanalytic Study of Male Homosexuals* (New York: Basic Books, 1962), 18.

2. For an excellent and balanced discussion of the intersection of the gay rights movement and American psychiatry, see R. Bayer, *Homosexuality and American Psychiatry* (New York: Basic Books, 1981), 102ff.

3. Ibid., 103.

4. Ibid.

5. Ibid., 105.

6. Karl Menninger, *Introduction to the Wolfenden Report* (New York: Stein & Day, 1963), 7.

7. Bayer, *Homosexuality*, 140.

8. Ibid., 141.

9. Ibid., 140.

10. Ibid., 141.

11. Ibid., 167.

12. George Orwell, "Politics and the English Language," in *Shooting An Elephant* (Harcourt Brace & Co., 1950).

13. E. Rueda, *The Homosexual Network* (Greenwich, Conn.: Devin-Adair Publishers, 1982).

14. Dennis Altman, "The Movement and Its Enemies," in *The Homosexualization of America* (Boston: Beacon Press, 1982), 112-13.

15. Carl B. Harding, "Letter," in *Mattachine Review*, August 1956, 35-36.

16. Altman, *Homosexualization of America*, 113.

17. Ibid.

18. See Anthony Cassano "Coming Out in the Churches," *Pastoral Renewal*, March 1981, 71-72.

19. Ibid.

20. See Duluth Human Rights Ordinance, Chapter 29C, Duluth City Code (1959 as amended).

21. The colloquy took place in an Advocates Debate on WCCO-TV on the Sunday before the vote on the St. Paul gay rights ordinance, 23 April 1978.

22. Such laws always provide serious civil penalties (see, for example, the Minneapolis Human Rights Ordinance, Minneapolis City Code, as amended). Some ordinances make it a criminal violation, holding out ninety days in jail as a possible penalty.

23. The only exception to the general right of landlords to rent to anyone they please is embodied in civil rights laws that protect unchangeable characteristics based on biology (sex, race), historical accident (national origin), or belief system (religion). None of these narrowly defined exceptions protects immoral behavior (see chapter 3).

Chapter Two

Who Are the Gays?
The Image and the Reality

*T*o understand whether gay rights laws make sense for society, we have to understand first who the gays are. The persuasiveness of claims against the rest of society can only be evaluated properly when we have defined and described who is making them. Here, as always, it is important to separate the image from the reality. The visitor at Wild West Village in Knott's Berry Farm can become so enchanted with the weather-worn wood, the dusty streets, and the smell of gunpowder that he altogether loses his orientation in time and space and never looks behind the elaborate facade. It is equally easy to lose perspective on public policy issues, to look merely at the carefully constructed image of the modern homosexual culture without examining the hard reality lurking behind the colorful exteriors.

Because demands for gay rights have profound social consequences, it is legitimate to examine the nature of "gayness" thoroughly before rushing to embrace it simply because it comes under the familiar and popular banner of equal rights. A spectrum of homosexual experience exists in society including (1) those who have a heterosexual orientation but who in particular situations—prison, adolescent experimentation, abuse—have had experiences of sexual contact with a member of the same sex; (2) those who have no sexual interest in members of the opposite sex but are not necessarily sexually active with those of the same sex; (3) those who have a compulsive desire for sexual contact with members of the same sex and act out that desire in promiscuous homosexual behavior; and (4) those who display some elements of homosexuality in practices such as transvestism (cross-dressing), bestiality, and other aberrant sexual behavior.

For many years, nearly all homosexuals remained in the closet, concealing their behavior from employers, from friends, even from spouses. Many wrestled against their impulses in much the same way an exhibitionist wrestles against the compulsive behavior that makes him feel guilty and ashamed. Such quiet, closeted, often tormented homosexuals rightfully evoke compassion from those who come to know their plight and would like to help them out of it. But these are not the people for whom the gay rights laws are primarily designed or who actively lobby for them. Because they keep their sexuality private, they are seldom, if ever, discriminated against. Content to stay outside the political arena, they are a group distinct from the militant homosexuals who want public acceptance, not just private tolerance, for their lifestyle.

The militant homosexual community has sought to overcome the natural revulsion their behavior triggers by efforts to polish their image, efforts that have been largely successful. They have won the support of many people of good will—including

prominent religious and political leaders—by identi-
fying themselves as an oppressed minority calling for
social justice. These leaders range from denominational
leaders of major religious groups to a coalition of
people who have been historical supporters of causes
associated with civil rights. Books have regularly
appeared to enlist, by firm or flimsy evidence, great
historical and literary figures in the homosexual camp,
frequently using bachelorhood, accusations of enemies,
ambiguous references in sonnets, or genuine same-sex
friendships to "establish" contributions made by
homosexuals to society.[1] Homosexuals often express an
interest in intellectual movements and the arts, a
worldly sophistication and a love for fashion. Some
militants suggest the spiritual or intellectual love of
same-sex partners is preferable to the more pedestrian
"breeding" of heterosexuals. Most of all, they want
their lifestyle to be seen as "gay," free from slavery to
conventional rules, exuberant, full of zest, and suffused
with commitment to loving, caring, and sharing
relationships. As one clinical psychiatrist summed up
the modern homosexual message: "See how
uninhibited we are, see how we've thrown off the
chains of guilt—unlike you poor straight people who
have for so long subjected us to feelings of
worthlessness and sinfulness."[2]

Against this idealized backdrop, it is useful to
examine more closely the realities of the modern
homosexual experience.

WHO ARE HOMOSEXUALS?

Homosexuals or *homophiles* seek orgasmic satisfaction from simulated sexual behavior with members
of the same sex rather than from normal sexual behavior with the opposite sex. Although some claim to be

bisexual in that they seek sexual gratification from both sexes, most do not engage in normal sexual behavior with the opposite sex.

WHAT DO HOMOSEXUALS DO?

Homosexuals typically engage in oral or anal sodomy, or mutual masturbation, with members of the same sex. Frustrated by the biological impossibility of natural sexual relations between members of the same sex, homosexuals must use body apertures not constructed for sexual penetration or bring their mouth into contact with areas designed for the elimination of human waste, either of which causes serious hygienic and health risks.[3]

Once the natural reluctance to come into contact with human waste is broken down, a significant proportion of homosexuals go further. Some homosexuals, such as the famous psychologist and sexologist Havelock Ellis, are urolagniacs, ingesting the urine and feces of their partners.[4] Although homosexuals have no monopoly on bizarre sexual practices, their initial attraction to unnatural acts draws them in disproportionate numbers to more widely known practices such as sadism and masochism, and less widely known (and better left undefined) practices such as fisting and rimming.

Homosexuals also practice other forms of deviant behavior. One book reports that one-fifth of all homosexuals admitted to having sexual contact, or at least masturbating, with animals.[5] A prominent homosexual, Charley Shively, wrote an article for *Fag Rag* titled "Bestiality as an Act of Revolution," and *The Gay Report*, a widely read and much praised book in the homosexual community, reports positive testimonials with no apparent shame and no adverse comment from those having sex with Labrador retrievers, cows, and horses: "My first sexual experience . . . was . . . with a cow—not bad but boys are better."[6] Most homosexuals have had some experience with oral-anal sex, sadomasochism, group orgies, bondage, or transvestism.[7]

WHERE DO HOMOSEXUALS DO IT?

Unlike the heterosexual, the male homosexual often practices his sexual behavior outside the privacy of his own bedroom. *Gayellow Pages*, a reference book widely circulated in the homosexual community, gives a state-by-state, city-by-city description of where homosexuals congregate and for what purpose. Letter codes reflect what is available: anal sex, oral sex, sadomasochism, and a bewildering variety of other perverse behavior. Several books have described the phenomenon and *The Gay Report* takes it as a given:

> It is generally well known that male homo-
> sexuals often perform sex outside the home.
> John Rechy's books, especially *Numbers* and
> *The Sexual Outlaw*, document the lives of sex
> hunters of city streets and parks. The use of
> public toilets for cruising and sex is so well
> known that a technical book by Cornell
> University entitled *The Bath Room* includes a
> whole section discussing the homosexual
> issue in the design of modern public
> restrooms. . . . Psychiatrists have on occasion
> suggested that men choose public places
> because they find the danger attractive. Most
> contemporary gay writers, however, indicate
> that sex in public places is chosen for its
> convenience or its anonymity or both, and a
> few have even suggested that there is

something revolutionary about both promiscuity and public sex.[8]

Frequent places mentioned for homosexual behavior are public restrooms at bus stations, service stations, shopping malls, public libraries, or rest stops (where visitors sometimes cut out circular "glory holes" in the partitions between the stalls for anonymous sex); public parks, such as areas in Golden Gate Park in San Francisco, where groups gather in the bushes according to their deviant specialty; beaches, where at designated times sodomites meet for furtive sexual activity; public baths or "health clubs," where groups gather around to watch others engage in sodomy or retire to private booths for one of a number of perverted acts; gay bars and nightclubs where homosexuals "cruise" each other, looking for short, ten-minute stands, often in the restrooms; street corners, where standing or signaling has special meaning for those cruising by in automobiles; and pornographic bookstores, peep shows, or movie houses, where small cubicles or lounge areas are used for sodomy or masturbation.[9]

Dr. Charles Socarides, a leading psychiatric expert on homosexuality, gives the flavor of such public liaisons: "Often the homosexual encounters consist of no more than a quick orgasm induced by two males grasping each other's genitals in the anonymous setting of a public toilet or darkened doorway."[10]

The baths in particular reveal much about homosexual practices:

> The degree of promiscuity in the baths defies the imagination of those not familiar with homosexuality. From the point of view of traditional values, they are probably some of the most destructive and degrading insti-

tutions in America today. There is no indica-
tion, however, that any of the homosexual
organizations has opposed or in any way
showed interest in counteracting the effects
of the baths. From the medical point of view,
the baths probably constitute a major focus
for the transmission of disease."

WITH WHOM DO HOMOSEXUALS DO IT?

Some homosexuals, of course, live desperately
lonely lives, punctuated by occasional and furtive
sexual behavior that leaves them feeling guilty and
ashamed. Others commit such acts only in their
tortured imaginations. A few (many of them women)
maintain, at least for a time, a longer-term relationship
with one partner. But these occasional practitioners are,
according to recent statistical data, dwarfed by their
more promiscuous brethren.

Until recently, the staggering promiscuity of the
homosexual community was only dimly appreciated
by the statisticians. A survey reported in the official
publication of the American Public Health Association,
for example, said that over a lifetime the typical
homosexual has forty-nine different sexual partners
and that between 8 percent and 12 percent of homosexuals have more than five hundred partners during
their lifetime.

Those numbers, though huge by heterosexual
standards, appear now to be the tip of the iceberg. A
fact long known within the homosexual community
was unveiled to the public only recently with the
fearful spread of a new disease. During the course of
research on AIDS, it was discovered that the typical
homosexual interviewed had over five hundred

different sexual partners. The AIDS victims considered by themselves averaged eleven hundred different sexual partners; some reported as many as twenty thousand.[12] Other reports showed that some homosexuals had as many as nine short sexual encounters in one evening at a bath or bar. One homosexual reported, "I believe my estimate of 4,000 sex partners to be very accurate. I have been actively gay since I was 13 (thirty-one years ago). An average of two or three new partners per week is not excessive, especially when one considers that I will have ten to twelve partners during one night at the baths."[13]

There is also widespread prostitution in the homosexual community. *The Advocate* shows the breadth of homosexual prostitution when it carries ads for "escort services"—as many as four hundred per issue. One observer estimated the total number of homosexual prostitutes in the United States at no fewer than seventy thousand. Another author estimated there are three hundred thousand boy prostitutes in the United States.[14]

The emphasis on youth and beauty, in a community without long-term monogamous commitment, leads inevitably to merchandising of sex as a commodity. One former homosexual describes his previous lifestyle:

> It was a sordid life. As you get older, anything good about homosexuality passes away and you are left with all of the bad things. You no longer are attractive and you cannot make contact. You have to pay for any sex you get. And then there is no involvement, there is no love. No friendship is involved; just a business transaction. So the rejection of the homosexual life is very intense.[15]

Although hotly contested by the homosexual community, substantial evidence indicates that homosexuals are also sexually involved with children. Some heterosexuals share the perverted practice, to be sure, but homosexuals have become increasingly open about it.[16] Since the decadent Roman wrote two millennia ago about the attractions of man-boy love, observers have noted linkages between homosexuality and pedophilia. The most prominent—and presumably most responsible—homosexuals, such as economist John Maynard Keynes, have sought out excursions to places where, as he put it, he could enjoy "bed and boy."[17] The Gay Teachers Association has demanded the right to teach students "gay is proud" and provide sexual "counseling."[18] New York homosexual teachers agreed that homosexual relationships with their students were improper, but reserved the right to have homosexual relations with other children outside the classroom.[19] Prominent homosexual activists and organizations have a stated objective to remove age-of-consent laws from state statutes, permitting voluntary sex with minors (see chapter 3). Los Angeles public schools have seen the introduction of Project 10 which, among other things, refers teenagers confused about their sexuality to homosexual counselors.

The coming out of the homosexual has also made public certain subgroups of the homosexual community. Homosexuals with tastes for interracial promiscuity founded "Black and White Men Together" (BWMT). The Eulenspiegel Society was formed for homosexuals drawn toward sadomasochism and perverse dominant/submissive sexual acts. The Eulenspiegel Society announced society meetings on "how to conduct a scene with a beginning masochist" and on "tattooing and dominant/submissive sex."[20]

A survey done by two homosexual authors revealed that three-fourths of homosexuals had at some time had sex with boys sixteen to nineteen or younger. One reported, "My lover and I are into young boys 13-18 years old. . . . I am actively involved with many of them insofar as the social services, family courts, schools, probation departments, etc. are concerned." Another said, "How long will we boy lovers have to wait? How long before we can walk honestly and proudly hand in hand with our young friends and not have to palm them off as our nephews or our stepsons?"[21]

One prominent homosexual activist told a group of educators that the homosexual has every right to influence children: "It is absurd to hire a teacher and then say 'But don't bring yourself to work. Don't bring your values or world view into the classroom.' "[22]

The interest in children by homosexual activists is reflected in this quotation from a speech at a North American Man/Boy Love Association meeting in Minneapolis: "There's not a boy out there . . . who does not need oral sex right now. I have never met a boy who did not enjoy being given oral sex."[23]

NAMBLA says it is "strongly opposed to age of consent laws and other restrictions which deny adults and youth the full enjoyment of their bodies and control over their lives." NAMBLA's goal is to end the long-standing oppression of men and boys involved in any mutually consensual relationship by (1) building a support network for such men and boys; (2) educating the public on the benevolent nature of man/boy love; (3) aligning with the lesbian, gay, and other movements for sexual liberation; and (4) supporting the liberation of persons of all ages from sexual prejudice and oppression.[24]

But such an interest is not limited to a lunatic fringe of homosexuals. Regrettably, prominent leaders have sexually used children. Perhaps the brightest judge on the Minnesota District Court bench, a Harvard Law School graduate, had to be removed from the bench for homosexual prostitution with minors.[25] A nationally celebrated artistic director in the children's theater movement was convicted a few years ago for repeated acts of child molestation, along with several of his associates. His conviction followed that of a prominent Minneapolis high school music teacher who repeatedly videotaped perverted sexual acts of minors, many of them his own students. And a superficial review of mainstream homosexual newspapers reveals advertisements such as the following:

> I'm wanting to establish a friendship with a 16-18 year old affectionate, gentle personality with a good sense of humor who would enjoy movies, breakfasts, music, skinny dipping, or biking with a clean, honest and caring 34-year-old male. Racial and economic background are not discriminating factors; no smoke or drugs, however.[26]

Such ads are not confined to the homosexual media. The *Minneapolis Star* several years ago carried an ad on its church page from a local homosexual church featuring a boy dressed only in shorts. It offered prizes and cash awards for homosexual adolescents who would come to a meeting at the church with examples of homosexual art or prose.

WHAT SPILLOVER EFFECTS DO HOMOSEXUALS HAVE ON SOCIETY?

Homosexual behavior leads to problems far beyond the circle of homosexuals themselves. As a group, homosexuals release both disease and crime into society to an extent far in excess of their percentage of the population.[27] The connection between homosexuals and ill health has been underscored most recently by the rise of AIDS.

Prior to this epidemic, however, the medical community had long known the medical effects of homosexuality. The high rate of illness in the homosexual community is legendary. One survey revealed that 78 percent of homosexuals have been affected at least once by a sexually transmitted disease (STD) and that a large number of homosexuals have been afflicted with illnesses such as urethritis, hepatitis, herpes, pediculosis, scabies, venereal warts, and intestinal parasites.[28]

Medical specialists know the disproportionate impact such diseases are having on the homosexual community. Although homosexuals represent 5 percent or less (homosexuals estimate 10 percent) of the U.S. population, they are responsible for half of the nation's cases of syphilis and a "phenomenal incidence of venereal disease" generally.[29] Syphilis, once thought under control, has recently burst into a new epidemic with a nationwide increase of 23 percent in the first six months of 1987 over the first six months of 1986, and a 105 percent increase over the same period in New York City alone.[30] Homosexuals also carry slightly more than half of the cases of gonorrhea of the throat and of intestinal infections.[31]

Diseased homosexual food handlers in public restaurants have been responsible for major outbreaks of amebiasis and hepatitis A infections in San Francisco and Minneapolis; homosexuals have a rate of infectious hepatitis B twenty to fifty times greater than heterosexual males, and significantly higher rates of hepatitis A.[32] Some studies show that between one-half and three-fourths of homosexual men have or have had hepatitis B.[33] Ninety percent of homosexually active men demonstrate chronic or recurrent viral infections with herpes virus, CMV, and hepatitis B.[34] It is no wonder that Dr. Selma Dritz, an official of the San Francisco Department of Public Health, wrote that "special precautions are required to protect the public from [disease carriers] who work as food handlers, bartenders, attendants in medical care facilities, and as teachers and aids in day-care centers for infants and young children."[35]

During the first decade that gay rights laws were in effect in San Francisco, the city saw a sharp increase in the venereal disease rate to twenty-two times the national average. Over a ten-year period the annual rate of infectious hepatitis A increased 100 percent; infectious hepatitis B, 300 percent; and amoebic colon infections increased 2,500 percent. Venereal disease clinics in the city saw seventy-five thousand patients every year during the same decade, of whom close to 80 percent were homosexual males. Twenty percent of them carried rectal gonorrhea.[36]

Homosexuals also have a group of rare bowel diseases, usually thought to be limited to the tropics. These are generally lumped together under the designation "gay bowel syndrome."[37] Because many male homosexuals ingest fecal matter, it is estimated that up to one-half have contracted parasitic amebiasis, a disease of the colon caused by parasites. One public official found 40 percent of homosexual men attending sexually transmitted disease clinics had the problem.[38] It is no wonder that the *New York Times Magazine* makes the following statement: "Bizarre infections are so common in the homosexual community that one scientist, presenting a report on these occurrences . . . called his talk 'Manhattan: The Tropical Isle.' "[39]

Such statistics do not come about by accident or bad luck. The physiology of the rectum makes it clear that sodomy is unnatural. The inward expansion of the rectum during anal intercourse frequently tears the rectal lining, resulting in spasms, colitis, cramps, and a variety of other physical responses.[40] Furthermore, sperm can readily penetrate the rectal wall (the vagina cannot be so penetrated) and do massive immunological damage, leaving the body vulnerable to a bewildering variety of opportunistic infections.[41] Simply put, homosexual practices are unhealthy.

The perilous combination of a disease-ridden population and incredible promiscuity led to the recent epidemic that has brought all these facts to public attention. Bursting into prominence in 1981, AIDS (Acquired Immune Deficiency Syndrome) soon had caused more fatalities than Legionnaires' disease and toxic shock syndrome combined. It was initially named GRID (Gay Related Immune Deficiency Disease), but whatever its acronym, it proved lethal. Fewer than 14 percent of AIDS victims have survived more than three years; no victim is known to have ever fully recovered.[42]

Early cases were identified almost simultaneously in January 1981 in New York, San Francisco, and Los Angeles. The first case was a thirty-one-year-old male model who arrived at UCLA with a severe fungal infection. Diagnosing him was difficult and he was treated as a victim of a rare infection. Soon, however, other unusual cases began turning up around the country, nearly all in homosexuals.[43] Finally the common cause was uncovered and the deadly new disease identified.

The medical community was confronted with a frightening prospect: a gruesome disease for which there was no known cure and a group of recklessly promiscuous carriers. The disease was horrible enough when confined to the homosexual community, but equally disturbing were increasing reports of the transmission of AIDS to innocent parties: to heterosexual partners of bisexuals, to hospital patients receiving transfusions of AIDS-contaminated blood, to hemophiliacs dependent on regular infusions of new blood for life, to infants born to mothers with AIDS. As syndicated columnist Patrick Buchanan described it:

> So long as AIDS appeared to be confined to active homosexuals, to a handful of Haitian refugees and to drug abusers using contaminated needles, there seemed no danger of a city-wide or national panic. It is now established, however, and becoming widely known, that AIDS can be transmitted through routine transfusion of blood donated by AIDS victims. The evidence: the rising toll among the nation's small population of hemophiliacs, among whom AIDS has become the second most common cause of death.[44]

Homosexuals and drug abusers are the largest segment of society affected, yet "given the fact that the virus is transmitted through sexual contact, through the traces of blood and needles and other drug paraphernalia and from mother to newborn infant, one can envision many possible chains of infection, which leave no segment of the U.S. population completely unaffected by the threat of AIDS."[45] Indeed, the fastest growing group of reported AIDS patients in 1988 was not adults but children.[46]

Worrisome to health care workers is the possibility that one can be infected with AIDS if blood penetrates skin or mucous membranes, a fact which represents a "small but definite occupational risk for health-care workers."[47]

AIDS will continue to be with us for some time. Extrapolation studies by the Public Health Service estimate that 1.5 million people in the U.S. are infected with HIV, the virus that causes AIDS. The best current evidence is that each one infected will eventually come down with the disease. Barring some cure, each one infected will die of AIDS. The model further predicts that 1990 will see an annual incidence of sixty thousand reported AIDS cases, up from thirty-nine thousand in 1988.[48] The cumulative case count should reach well over three hundred thousand by the end of 1992.[49] Experts are talking of a second great wave of AIDS infections in the inner city, riding a crest of hardcore drug use and sexual promiscuity. C. Everett Koop, former surgeon general, now says:

> Everything that turns up confirms heterosexual spread, numerically and geographically. . . . Most recent estimates are that there will be, in the year 2000, a hundred million people who are HIV-positive.[50]

It is no wonder that AIDS has replaced cancer as the nation's most feared disease. Although there have been some concerns that AIDS might break out into the general population, the possibility of the breakout foreseen by Dr. Koop is still a matter of some controversy among medical scholars.

The best evidence now is that heterosexuals have not been at substantial risk for contracting AIDS simply because they do not commit the sexual acts most closely linked with efficient AIDS transmission. While all agree AIDS has spread among heterosexuals, not all agree that the spread will be substantial. The

Centers for Disease Control's chief epidemiologist, Dr. Harold Jaffe, has said: "Those who are suggesting that we are going to see an explosive spread of AIDS in the heterosexual population have to explain why this isn't happening."[51]

Even though a measure of controversy surrounds the future scope of the AIDS epidemic, one thing is not controversial. Homosexuals have been the principal recipients and transmitters of the AIDS virus—70 percent of all AIDS cases have occurred in homosexuals; in some states and in Europe, the percentages are even higher.[52]

Why are homosexuals the principal victims of AIDS? The answer is not complicated. With sexually transmitted AIDS, the overwhelming risk factor is anal intercourse, especially for the passive or recipient partner. According to B. Frank Polk, director of the Johns Hopkins University's component of the Multicenter AIDS Cohort Study, "In gay men, 95% or more of the infections occur from receptive anal intercourse."[53] And the *American Journal of Public Health* reported that in one study of 240 men who became infected with AIDS, all but four had engaged in anal sex as a receptor.[54]

An additional cause, of course, is the incredible level of homosexual promiscuity:

> Lately, thanks to AIDS, the word "promiscuity" has begun to acquire an unfavorable connotation among homosexuals, but not so long ago it was carried as a badge of honor, if not a defining condition of homosexuality itself. It is certainly a defining characteristic of AIDS sufferers.[55]

Even at the beginning of the developing crisis in 1985, 69 percent of men having three or more sexual partners the previous month agreed with the statement "It is hard to change my sexual behavior because being gay means doing what I want sexually."[56] So far, therefore, the principle purveyors and victims of AIDS have been homosexuals themselves.

HOMOSEXUALS AND VIOLENT CRIME

Such spillover effects of homosexuality are not, however, limited to health. Some observers have noted a connection between homosexuality and crimes of violence. One study by a long-time and somewhat controversial antagonist of homosexuality suggested that homosexuals are fifteen times more likely to commit murder than nonhomosexuals. The report alleges that this stereotype is so pervasive that among police, gory murders are assumed to be homosexual until proven otherwise. "It would appear plausible that those who are missocialized in an area as important as sexuality would also be more likely to be missocialized in their treatment of human life."[57] Such a connection may be more causal than accidental, more a pattern than an occasional John Gacy, the Chicago contractor who murdered scores of adolescents and buried them in his basement. Indeed, approximately one out of ten homicides in San Francisco is the result of sado-masochistic sex among homosexuals.[58]

As frightening as the statistics is the nonchalant way such violence is handled in the homosexual press. Typical is an *Equal Time* report of a rally on January 6, 1984, in the heart of a homosexual residential neighborhood in San Francisco. The report describes the rally without apparent disapproval. At the rally, some nine thousand people protested the release of Dan White, the San Francisco city council member who shot to death George Moscone, the mayor, and an openly homosexual city council member, Harvey Milk. White was found guilty only of voluntary manslaughter by a twelve-member jury. The keynote speaker at the rally was "Sister Boom-Boom," one of a group of drag-queen "nuns" called the Sisters of Perpetual Indulgence. The "Sisters" appear around San Francisco dressed as nuns with a flagrantly homosexual flavor. The crowd, stirred to a frenzy by Sister Boom-Boom, heard him say that Councilman White's days were numbered: "Yesterday was the last day Dan White could spend knowing that he would live through the day. Today, Dan White begins a life sentence, and I'm sorry to say I don't think it's going to be a long one." As the speeches went on, men tossed black "Dan White Hit Squad" buttons over the crowd. Buttons were quickly grabbed and pinned on dozens of shirts and jackets. Thousands in the crowd sang along with a rendition of "Oh, Danny Boy," singing "Oh, Danny, where you gonna go? Someone's gonna find you, wherever you go."[59]

ARE HOMOSEXUALS BORN THAT WAY?

Although gay rights laws customarily speak of "affectional preference," homosexuals on the defensive frequently say they have no choice. Responsibility for sexual practices is shuffled to one side by claims that homosexuals are born that way or merely discover and affirm what they are naturally, and they cannot change their nature. On such points, the factual evidence is increasingly clear.

Although an early study suggested a biological reason for homosexuality, nearly all modern analysts support the conclusion that homosexuals are not born that way. They learn to be that way:

The question is often asked if there is not some kind of genetic or hormonal factor, innate or inborn, which accounts for this condition. Homosexuality, the choice of a partner of the same sex for orgastic satisfaction, is not innate. There is no connection between sexual instinct and the choice of sexual object. Such an object choice is learned, acquired behavior: there is no inevitable genetically inborn propensity towards the choice of a partner of either the same or opposite sex.[60]

A famous radio personality, exposed for homosexual activity, purportedly said he could not help it because it "is in my genes." Modern medicine has confirmed that this is not the case. As Dr. James McCary, author of *Sexual Myths and Fallacies*, points out: "Neither present day endocrinological tests nor microscopic or clinical examinations have revealed any physiological differences between the heterosexual and homosexual individual."[61]

Even where that is conceded, however, some might argue that homosexual orientation is acquired so early in life that it might as well be genetic. If it is determined by age three or four and permanently fixed, one can argue, it can be regarded as involuntary or immutable.

That analysis ignores two things. Even if propensity to homosexuality is acquired early, that does not distinguish homosexuality from a variety of other tendencies which may afflict people early on. Psychologists may discern a bent to steal, to be abusive, or to rebel quite early in life. Those inclinations—what religious people might call temptations— if nurtured may develop into hardened behavioral practices. But it would be strange for a thief to claim protected status of the civil rights laws because his inclination to steal began early in life and has now hardened into an immutable lifestyle. Second, there is substantial evidence that homosexuals can change wherever there is a willingness to change (a subject to be explored more fully in the next section).

Homosexuals do not simply discover an alternative, perfectly normal form of sexual behavior somehow natural to them. They acquire, through a variety of decisions, influences, and choices, a vulnerability toward, and later a pattern of, behavior that is disordered and dangerous. Dr. Armand Nicholai, chief psychiatrist of the Medical School at Harvard University and editor of *The Harvard Guide to Psychiatry*, said:

> I have treated hundreds of homosexuals. None of them, deep down, thought he was normal. Simulating eating is not eating. Simulating being female is not being female. Simulating sex is not sex.[62]

As another prominent psychiatrist put it:

> Those who urge the acceptance of homosexuality as simply a normal form of sexuality, rather than a behavioral disorder, developmental arrest or failure, or a clinical illness, reflect the blurred boundaries of social behavior which currently impair communal health in many ways.[63]

In whatever way the desires become implanted, some homosexuals choose to act on them. And while "preference" fits better with the "gay" myth of liberation, the "born that way" argument fits better with the political needs of the movement. And so some continue to use ambiguous tests, explainable either by environmental or genetic factors, to contradict the overwhelming consensus that homosexuality is a learned behavior.

The reason is apparent. If homosexuality is natural, doing homosexual acts becomes an accepted solution to relieve pent-up—and now natural—drives. Unfortunately, the solution never works, disproving the natural explanation:

> The "solution" of homosexuality is always doomed to failure and, even when used for utilitarian purposes—for example, financial benefits when being supported by a partner—is characterized by strife and turmoil. Homosexuality is . . . filled with destruction and self-deceit. It is a masquerade of life in which certain psychic energies are neutralized and held in a marginally quiescent state. However, the unconscious manifestations of hate, destructiveness, incest, and fear always threaten to break through. Instead of union, cooperation, solace, stimulation, emotional enrichment, and a maximum opportunity for creative interpersonal maturation and realistic fulfillment, there are multiple underlying factors which constantly threaten any ongoing homosexual relationship: destruction, mutual defeat, exploitation of the partner and the self, oral-sadistic incorporation, aggressive onslaughts, and attempts to alleviate anxiety—all comprising a pseudo-solution to the aggressive and libidinal conflicts that dominate and torment the individuals involved.[64]

CAN HOMOSEXUALS CHANGE?

Whether homosexuals can change their orientation is, for some, a key argument in the gay rights debate. That, of course, is not the only issue. Even if homosexual orientation were unchangeable, that would not mean that homosexual activity must continue. But if homosexuals cannot change their orientation, it makes their analogy to other civil rights groups more compelling.

Some early psychiatric opinion suggested that change in sexual orientation was rarely feasible. Recent studies have shown, however, that homosexuality need not be a permanent condition. Homosexuals can change.[65] The key is whether they want to.

The purported unchangeableness of the homosexual is belied by findings of traditional psychotherapists. Irving Bieber's study of seventy-two patients revealed that 38 percent had become heterosexuals or bisexuals and 27 percent had shifted from homosexuality and bisexuality to exclusive heterosexuality.[66] Sex therapists William Masters and Virginia Johnson found, after a fifteen-year study, that they were successful in helping two-thirds of the men and women who indicated a desire to become exclusively heterosexual.[67] One psychiatric survey concludes that "psychotherapy appears to be unsuccessful in only a small number of patients of any age in whom a long habit is combined with . . . lack of desire to change."[68]

When homosexuality is viewed as a behavior rather than as an identity, it can be changed using basic psychological counseling techniques. Without underestimating the struggle required to break such a deeply ingrained and habitual sexual pattern, the recent evidence of successful transformations into

normal sexual patterns is too substantial to ignore.
Both Christian organizations and secular psychiatrists
have accumulated substantial clinical evidence that the
homosexual can change—with adequate support, encouragement, and motivation.[69]

This evidence contradicts the popular lore that
"once gay, always gay." Until the 1930s and 1940s, the
same pessimism infected popular attitudes about
drunkards. They were seen as hopeless derelicts and a
burden to society. Now no sensible person doubts that
alcoholics can and do recover, and gain or regain a
useful place in society.

During the past decade a variety of groups, both
religious and secular, have emerged to demonstrate the
truth of their conviction that homosexuals can change.
These groups are making advances into territory not
previously explored. Their endurance suggests a hopeful
future. Some, like Homosexuals Anonymous, are
patterned directly after Alcoholics Anonymous. The best
of these groups have one thing in common: they
emphasize the importance of personal responsibility for
change, learning to make responsible choices with the
help of others.

What alcoholics learned is that an honest "coming
out," without excuses or rationalizations but with a
sincere desire to change, is a powerful tool for success.
They found that a humble declaration of need evokes
not just compassion but respect from others. That same
reservoir of good will and helpfulness awaits the
humble homosexual who wants to change.

Homosexuals can change. But they need to understand that their behavior is unacceptable. Just as it
would be ludicrous to call for alcoholic's rights or to
have a day celebrating drunkenness, it is equally
ludicrous to call for gay rights legislation or to have a

day celebrating perversion. The alcoholic discovers in AA that the fault is not with others (society, wife, boss) but with himself; likewise the responsibility for change lies not with others, but with himself. Those enablers who accepted him—made up excuses for his absence from work, explained away the bruises he left on children, rationalized his behavior as inherited—were facilitating his collapse. So too the public acceptance of homosexuality expressed in gay rights laws and gay pride days provides an easy way out for those who want to appear tolerant and loving, but in actuality it promotes conduct destructive to the homosexual himself.

HOW SHOULD WE TREAT HOMOSEXUALS?

To understand the gay rights issue, it has been necessary to describe the lifestyle of the modern homosexual. Much of the statistical information has come from surveys done by homosexuals themselves. The bizarre practices that have been uncovered, including some of the more extreme and eccentric behaviors, show the kinds of activity given special protection by gay rights legislation.

In describing homosexual behavior, of course, it has been necessary to generalize. There are homosexual men and women who are less promiscuous than average, who seldom (or never) engage in sexual practices in public places, who practice less exotic forms of perversion, and who live relatively conventional lives. Wherever they may fall in the continuum of homosexual experience, however, these people are entitled to all the freedoms and protections of our system of law without exception.

Homosexuals are made, not born. They are responsible for their conduct. But no person of good will should use this as a justification for personal acts of cruelty, violence, or insult. On a personal as well as legal basis, homosexuals are entitled to respect as human beings, as persons with immortal souls. But this respect does not require the provision of special privileges that would infringe on the rights or liberties of others. A concern for homosexuals as people will lead, paradoxically, to withholding social acceptance of their behavior.

Chapter 2, Notes

1. See, for example, J. Katz, *Gay American History* (New York: Thomas Crowell, 1976); M. Friedman and M. Rubin, *American Educator* 67 (1978), which claims, among others, Michelangelo and Alexander the Great. Homosexuals are on good ground when they claim Oscar Wilde or Walt Whitman, but stretch to include others on little evidence. They claim, for example, the ancient Greek writers for their admiration of the beauty of young boys without pointing out that sexual contact with them was a capital offense in ancient Athens. A good example of overreaching the evidence is the case of Michelango. He is widely accused of homosexuality based on two things: his bachelorhood and allegations brought against him by Aretino, a notorious blackmailer. As Irving Stone, author of *The Agony and the Ecstacy*, a famous biography of Michelangelo, points out, "We did not find a scintilla of evidence to support the allegation that Michelangelo was a homosexual." Letter from Irving Stone to Abigail Van Buren, *Washington Star*, 20 April 1981.

2. Paul Walker, quoted in N. Meredith, "The Gay Dilemma," *Psychology Today*, January 1984, 60. This is also a common theme in homosexual publications such as *The Advocate*, *GLC Voice*, and *Equal Time* (the first a nationwide magazine, the last two Minneapolis-St. Paul area tabloid newspapers).

3. The health risks of homosexuality are nowhere more clearly seen than in the AIDS epidemic. See "The AIDS Epidemic," *Newsweek*, 18 April 1983, 74–79; Glenn Wood and John Dietrich, *The AIDS Epidemic* (Portland, Ore.: Multnomah Press, 1990).

4. See Zygmund Dobbs, *Keynes at Harvard* (New York: Veritas Press, 1963); A. Calder Marshall, *The Sage of Sex* (New York: Putnam, 1959); H. Ellis, *Studies in the Psychology of Sex* (New York: Random House, 1942).

5. See F. DuMas, *Gay Is Not Good* (Nashville: Thomas Nelson Publishers, 1979).

6. K. Jay and A. Young, *The Gay Report* (New York: Summit, 1979), 567.

7. Ibid., 553-96, 490-93.

8. Ibid., 500.

9. Ibid., 501; see also *Gayellow Pages*.

10. Charles Socarides, "Homosexuality: Basic Concepts and Psychodynamics," *International Journal of Psychiatry* 10 (March 1972): 119. For other psychiatric references, see I. Bieber et al., *Homosexuality* (New York: Basic Books, 1962); H. Gershman, "Psychopathology of Compulsive Homosexuality," *American Journal of Psychoanalysis* 17 (1957): 58-77; Edward Glover, *The Roots of Crime: Selected Papers on Psychoanalysis*, vol. 2 (London: Imago Publishing Co., 1960); S. Hadden, "What Outcome Can Be Expected in Psychotherapy of Homosexuals," *Medical Aspects of Human Sexuality* 5 (December 1971): 96-100; M. Mahler, "On Human Symbiosis and Vicissitudes of Individuation," *Journal of the American Psychoanalytic Association* 15 (1967): 740-63.

11. E. Rueda, *The Homosexual Network* (Greenwich, Conn.: Devon-Adair Publishers, 1982), 37.

12. Study, U.S. Centers for Disease Control (Atlanta, 1982), reported in Meredith, "The Gay Dilemma," 56. See also A. Bell and M. Weinberg, *Homosexualities* (New York: Simon & Shuster, 1978), 85-86.

13. Jay and Young, *Gay Report*, 250.

14. See figures in Rueda, *Homosexual Network*, 181-85.

15. Interview in C. Philpot, *The Gay Theology* (Plainfield, N.J.: Logos, 1977), 23.

16. The evidence is clear from such movements as the North American Man/Boy Love Association and the support of homosexual groups for elimination of laws governing minimum ages of consent for sexual acts. See also DuMas, *Gay Is Not Good*, 105-6.

17. See Dobbs, *Keynes at Harvard*; Marshall, *Sage of Sex*; Ellis, *Psychology of Sex*.

18. "Bill of Rights," Gay Teachers Association, July 1977.

19. "Homosexual Love Away from School Is OK, Gay Teachers Say," *New York Post*, 11 July 1979.

20. Rueda, *Homosexual Network*, 73.

21. Jay and Young, *Gay Report*, 275, 279, 281.

22. *Gay Community News*, quoting a speech by Virginia Apuzzo, executive director of the National Gay Rights Task Force, to two hundred educators at Harvard, 23 April 1983.

23. "Child Molesters Picketed," *Twin Cities Christian*, 5 July 1984.

24. Rueda, *Homosexual Network*, 175.

25. The removal was affirmed unanimously by the Minnesota Supreme Court. *State Board* v. *Winton*, NW 2d (Minn. 1984).

26. *GLC Voice* Classifieds, 18 July 1984, 13.

27. See Rueda, *Homosexual Network*. See generally P. Buchanan and J. Muir, "Gay Times and Diseases," *The American Spectator*, August 1984, 15-18.

28. Rueda, *Homosexual Network*, 52-53. See also T. Quinn, "The Polymicrobial Origin of Intestinal Infections in Homosexual Men," *New England Journal of Medicine* 309 (1983):576-82; David Ostrow et

al., eds., *Sexually Transmitted Diseases in Homosexual Men* (New York: Plenum Medical Book Co., 1982); L. Corey and K. Holmes, "Sexual Transmission of Hepatitis A in Homosexual Men," *New England Journal of Medicine* 302 (1980):435-38; Gerald Mandell et al., eds., *Principles and Practice of Infectious Diseases*, 3rd ed. (New York: John Wiley and Sons, 1990), 2280-84, and references therein.

29. Katie Leishman, "AIDS and Syphilis," *The Atlantic Monthly*, January 1988, 20, 21.

30. Ibid.

31. E. Rowe, *Homosexual Politics* (CLA, 1984), 17.

32. Buchanan and Muir, "Gay Times and Diseases," 17, 18. The remarkable incidence of hepatitis in homosexual men is noted throughout medical literature. See Corey and Holmes, "Hepatitis A in Homosexual Men"; Mandell et al., *Infectious Diseases*, 2280-84 and references therein.

33. J. Kassler, *Gay Mens' Health* (New York: Harper and Row, 1983), 38.

34. Ostrow et al., *Diseases in Homosexual Men*, 204.

35. See Buchanan and Muir, "Gay Times," 18.

36. See generally, *San Jose Mercury News*, 24 April 1980; "Sharp Increase in Hepatitis and Dysentery in San Francisco," *San Francisco Chronicle Examiner*, 23 April 1979; see also "The Advocate Guide to Gay Health" (1983); Mandell et al., *Infectious Diseases*, 2280-84 and references therein.

37. Ostrow et al., *Diseases in Homosexual Men*, 204.

38. Ibid.

39. Henig, "AIDS: A New Disease's Deadly Odyssey," *New York Times Magazine*, 6 February 1983.

40. Ostrow et al., "Hemorrhoids, Anal Fissure, and Condylomata Acuminata," *Diseases in Homosexual Men*, 141-49.

41. G. Manligit et al., "Chronic Immune Stimulation by Sperm Alloantigens," *Journal of the American Medical Association* 251 (1984):237-41. See also J. Richards et al., "Rectal Insemination Modifies Immune Responses in Rabbits," *Science* 224 (1984):390-92; G. Shearer and A. Rabson, "Semen and AIDS," *Nature* 308 (1984):230.

42. "The AIDS Epidemic," *Newsweek*, 18 April 1983, 74. See also G. Ahronheim, "The Transmission of AIDS," *Nature* 313 (1985):534; R. T. Ravenholt, "Role of Hepatitis B Virus in Acquired Immunodeficiency Syndrome," *Lancet* (1983): 885-86; W. Winkelstein et al., "Potential for Transmission of AIDS-Associated Retrovirus from Bisexual Men in San Francisco to Their Female Sexual Contacts," *Journal of the American Medical Association* 255 (1986):901; H. Jaffe et al., "National Case-Control Study of Kaposis Sarcoma and *Pneumocystis Carinii* Pneumonia in Homosexual Men," *Annals Internal Medicine* 99 (1983):145-57; Mandell et al., *Infectious Diseases*, 2280-84 and references therein.

43. Ibid. Other groups affected include intravenous drug users, hemophiliacs, and, more recently, heterosexual partners of bisexuals.

44. Patrick Buchanan, "AIDS, Homosexuals and Political Dynamite," *Washington Times*, 1 June 1983, 2C.

45. W. Heyward and J. Curran, "The Epidemiology of AIDS in the U.S." *Scientific American*, October 1988, 72. The entire issue is devoted to "what science knows about AIDS."

46. Ibid., 78.

47. Ibid., 79. Heyward and Curran also report that transfusion of a single unit of HIV-contaminated blood is "very likely to result in infection" (p. 79).

48. Ibid., 81.

49. Ibid. See also Helene M. Cole and George D. Lundberg, eds., *AIDS from the Beginning* (Chicago: American Medical Association, 1986); G. P. Wormser et al., *AIDS (Acquired Immune Deficiency Syndrome) and Other Manifestations of HIV Infection* (Park Ridge, N.J.: Noyes Publications, 1987).

50. P. Dean, "America's New Family Doctor," *Minneapolis Star Tribune*, 24 November 1989, 29A.

51. M. Fumento, "AIDS: Are Heterosexuals at Risk?" *Commentary* 84 (November 1987):22.

52. See Heyward and Curran, "Epidemiology of AIDS," 78.

53. Fumento, "AIDS," 22-23.

54. Ibid., 23.

55. Ibid.

56. L. McKusick et al., "AIDS and Sexual Behavior Reported by Gay Men in San Francisco" *American Journal of Public Health* 75 (1985):493-96.

57. P. Cameron, "Report on Homosexuality and Murder," Institute for the Scientific Investigation of Sexuality (1984). Cameron found the murder rate to be fifteen times higher for homosexuals. While there are heterosexual Richard Specks as well as homosexual John Gacys, Cameron reports a disproportionate percentage of homosexual mass murders. Cameron is a controversial researcher whose views and research are frequently questioned by homosexuals, by the American Psychological Association, and by the American Sociological Association, with which Dr. Cameron has had long-standing controversies. The latter associations explicitly endorse gay rights measures.

58. "Coroner Battles Sado-masochistic Injuries," *Associated Press*, 12 March 1981. See also *Blade*, 11 September 1981.

59. *Equal Time*, 25 January 1984, 3.

60. Socarides, "Homosexuality," 118. See also T. Hoult, "Human Sexuality in Biological Perspective: Theoretical and Methodological Considerations," *Journal of Homosexuality* 9 (Winter 1983):137-55.

61. J. McCary, *Sexual Myths and Fallacies* (New York: Van Nostrand Reinhold, 1971), 94.

62. Personal conversation with the author.

63. Socarides, "Homosexuality," 120.

64. Ibid, 119.

65. Ibid, 123-24.

66. Rueda and Schwartz, *Gays, AIDS and You*, 72.

67. Ibid.

68. Socarides, "Homosexuality," 124.

69. Many people trying to escape from homosexuality could benefit from the help of a support group. The secular group Homosexuals Anonymous has chapters across the nation. Exodus International is an educational organization that gives referrals to Christian support groups around the world (P. O. Box 2121, San Rafael, CA 94912, (415) 454-1017).

Chapter Three

What Are Gay Rights?
The Legal Implications of Gay Rights Ordinances

G eorgetown University is a traditional Roman Catholic school with a strong reputation for academic excellence and a staunch commitment to Roman Catholic moral teaching. Located in Washington, D.C., the university is subject to the laws of the municipality. Among those laws is the District of Columbia Human Rights Ordinance, enacted in 1981, which forbids discrimination in the use of public facilities on the basis of "sexual orientation."[1]

Proponents of the measure, in Washington as elsewhere, had emphasized that it would not be construed to interfere with sincerely held religious views. And so when the Law Center, the university law school, saw the organization of a "Gay Rights Coalition," the university refused to recognize it or permit it to use university facilities to promote sexual behavior that is immoral and perverted according to historic Roman Catholic doctrine. The university argued that it was constitutionally entitled to the free exercise of its religious beliefs under the First

Amendment and should not be compelled to sacrifice its convictions and violate its conscience by allowing its facilities to be used to affirm unnatural sexuality.

The Gay Rights Coalition sued based on the ordinance. The court thus had to determine which claim had priority: the constitutional right to free exercise of religion or the D.C. Human Rights Act. The court decided that the "compelling government interest" in eliminating discrimination based on sexual orientation outweighed the interference with the university's religious convictions and compelled the university to open its facilities for teachings antithetical to its religious faith.[2]

The result was a clear signal to churches and church-related organizations and institutions as well as to individuals with religious or moral convictions on homosexuality. When a bona fide religious conviction collides with a gay rights ordinance, the constitutionally protected conviction may give way.

But as troubling as this decision are some of the near misses.

In 1977, a young man in Minneapolis presented himself to the Big Brothers organization, which attempts to introduce fatherless boys to men who would make exemplary role models for them. Given the increasing number of single parent families, Big Brothers organizations throughout the country have experienced an expanding list of mothers who request Big Brothers—men to take their sons fishing, camping, hiking, and to other recreational activities the mother may be unable to provide. The applicant on this day was eager to become a Big Brother.

While reviewing the applicant's resume during the interview, the Big Brothers representative noticed several items that suggested homosexual affiliations. He asked the applicant whether he was a homosexual.

The man admitted he was. Despite this revelation, the interview was not terminated. The interviewer mentioned that Big Brothers had a policy of revealing all they knew about potential Big Brothers to the mothers of their clients. Clients had the last word on the suitability of any applicant. It would work the same way with this revelation, the interviewer pointed out. If the mother had no objections to his homosexuality, he would be a Big Brother. It was her "right" either way.

A liberal policy, you might think. But it was not enough for the man who wanted to be a Big Brother. He immediately sued under the Minneapolis gay rights ordinance, alleging that he had been discriminated against as a homosexual. The mere fact that his homosexuality was made known to the mother, he argued, would likely lead to his disqualification as a Big Brother. He was thus being discriminated against for his affectional preference. Big Brothers argued there was nothing discriminatory about this policy. It made no comments, negative or positive, about him. Its representative simply revealed all the facts, just as he would with other protected classes in the human rights law—race, color, age, religion, sex, marital status, and the like. The decision was left up to the mother.

Despite the fair-sounding rationale of Big Brothers, the human rights hearing officer in Minneapolis found Big Brothers guilty of discrimination under the ordinance. Based on that finding, the claimant's lawyer asked for what the law entitled him to: thousands of dollars in costs, the acceptance of the homosexual as part of the organization without disclosing his homosexual preference to mothers of the sons who might go off on weekend outings with him, and "affirmative action," an active solicitation of homosexuals by Big Brothers in the homosexual media.

Mixed among the ads soliciting homosexual partners would be advertisements for Big Brothers in Minneapolis, seeking to entice the readership to come to Big Brothers in Minneapolis and be a "big brother" to Minneapolis boys. Before this shoe could drop, Big Brothers brought action in state district court. Although the result was by no means a foregone conclusion, given the vaguely worded ordinance, the judge randomly assigned to the case agreed with Big Brothers and reversed the finding of discrimination. But the case cost the nonprofit organization thousands of dollars. Rather than run the gauntlet again, Big Brothers gave in. They announced in the fall of 1983 that they now have a "national policy of accepting 'gay' men as prospective brothers to fatherless youth, 6-16 years old, unless the man is 'unstable' or has a 'poor life style.' "

At approximately the same time, Father Buchanan, a Roman Catholic priest in St. Paul, was interviewing candidates for eighth grade music teacher at Holy Childhood School. A candidate listed past school employment in music and, based on his resume, seemed qualified. The priest's suspicions were raised, however, when the man insisted he wanted to teach boys. Further research revealed that he was a homosexual. The decision for the priest was easy—his religious convictions and prudence dictated that he not permit a homosexual on the faculty.

Again, the candidate sued, this time under the St. Paul gay rights ordinance which was identical to the one in Minneapolis. The human rights agency made a preliminary determination of discrimination; the file had been turned over to the St. Paul city attorney for criminal prosecution, with possible sanctions including a ninety-day jail sentence and a three hundred dollar fine, when the St. Paul voters overwhelmingly repealed the gay rights ordinance. Like many similar ordinances around the country, the St. Paul ordinance, once put before the voters, lost by a landslide.

More recently, in Madison, Wisconsin, Ann Hacklander and Maureen Rowe were renting an apartment and looking for a roommate to share the expense. When Cari Sprague expressed an interest in living with them and disclosed she was a lesbian, they told her politely they would prefer someone else. Sprague took the matter immediately to the Madison Equal Opportunities Commission (MEOC), an agency charged with enforcement of the Madison gay rights law.

MEOC summoned Hacklander and Rowe to a meeting that proved to be a four-and-a-half hour self-criticism session. Reduced to tears at the meeting, Hacklander later said she "felt like [she] was in China," not the United States. The result of the meeting was an agreement exacted by MEOC. The two women would pay Sprague fifteen hundred dollars, would attend a sensitivity training class taught by homosexuals, would have their housing situation monitored by MEOC for two years, and would apologize to Sprague in a formal letter. When Rowe, a recent graduate, claimed the settlement would bankrupt her, she was told her bankruptcy was of no consequence to MEOC.

The city council later amended the law so it would not apply to roommate situations, but MEOC continued to lumber along with its case against the two women anyway, knowing that even if Hacklander and Rowe were ultimately to win, they would still have lost in attorney's fees, stress, and time.

These near misses, along with the one direct hit on constitutional liberties, reflect a harsh reality about legal solutions to political problems. They are always, universally, coercive. They start innocently with theoretical discussions of liberty and equality and end, like the French revolution, with the guillotine. The principle put into practice leads to an inevitable development of case-by-case resolutions that may end with a priest behind bars, a charitable organization wondering whether it ought to close its doors, or some roommates in a college town reduced to tears (and worse) for not wanting to share their apartment with a lesbian.

This is not, of course, a good argument for anarchy. Some issues are so important to the social and political fabric of the country that society tolerates the accompanying coercion. Society is willing to coerce people into keeping their fists off other people's noses and their fingers off other people's wallets. But before society exercises its coercive power to override bona fide religious convictions and historic rights, like the right of a parent to exercise discretion in overseeing the moral character of those who come into contact with her child, there had better be substantial justification. As Abraham Lincoln once said, "What I call liberty is allowing people the maximum freedom in the things they own and the things they do, as long as they do not interfere with the rights of others to do the same."

When it comes to gay rights, therefore, the proponents of such legislation have the burden of proof to show that it is necessary, and it is a heavy burden. From a review of the debates in Congress, in state legislatures, and in city councils, those proponents have yet to make a substantial case.

THE DEVELOPMENT OF GAY RIGHTS PROPOSALS

In the last two decades, gay rights activists have begun to press a new, radically different set of claims to civil rights protection. Human rights statutes historically have granted special legal standing to those "discrete and insular minorities"[3] who share an immutable *status*. That status was generally unrelated to behavior, traditional perceptions of moral character, or public health. One's racial inheritance, for example, creates a true *status*. Race tells us nothing about a person's lifestyle or behavior. Removing race as a criterion of social decision making therefore makes sense to all but the most arbitrary decision maker.

Gay rights proposals redefine status without ever saying so. Rather than acknowledge that such laws protect a social behavior (say, the commission of anal sodomy) whose benefits or detriments to society must be objectively evaluated before the protection is given, proponents create a new minority status. An uncritical acceptance of that new status derails a rational inquiry into the underlying behavior and disguises the fact that this minority is bound together by sexual activity—a common inclination to commit sodomy with members of the same sex. This new status group, given a new name ("gay") which itself begs the question of whether the group shares a common nature or a common behavior, has been proposed as worthy of legal protection under human rights laws extended to include "sexual preference" or "sexual orientation."

This jump from true status to behavior-based status creates the potential for innumerable protected classes ranging from sexual to recreational behaviors, from serious to frivolous interests, from committed involvements to take-it-or-leave-it hobbies. How does one decide, for example, whether to protect classes of such demographic variety as smokers, philatelists, spelunkers, adulterers, lepidopterists, bikers, or law review contributors?

This does not mean that no behavior-based status can ever be the subject of special legal privileges or protections. It only suggests that behavior-based status must be analyzed differently—and far more cautiously—than true status. Good public policy demands that sensible judgments be made on the behavior which will be given special status. Civil rights ought not to be created by classification. That is political nominalism. To create a behavior-based status and endow it *ex opere operato* (that is, by the mere act of creating such a status) with civil rights begs the question. One must ask the right questions. Is this a behavior worthy of special status? What is its impact on society, on those who practice it? Is it morally neutral—at least from the standpoint of conventional and sincerely held moral systems?

The moral force of the civil rights movement has caused many to make this jump uncritically, to treat gay rights as desirable and undistinguishable from the claims made for true status. Two states and approximately fifty other municipalities now prohibit discrimination against homosexuals under general human rights provisions.[4] Certain states prohibit discrimination against homosexuals in more narrow settings, such as public housing. Other states have executive orders that prohibit some forms of discrimination against homosexuals.

Most of these ordinances have been enacted by analogizing homosexual behavior to a true status. By adopting a status word not descriptive of their behavior ("gay"), homosexuals have successfully deflected attention from conduct some statutes still describe as the "abominable and detestable crime against nature," causing many to accept uncritically their minority status. The success of the analogy is reflected both by the ordinances cited above and by a smattering of judicial decisions. Some respected judges have found the analogy attractive. Justice Tobriner, writing for the California Supreme Court in *Gay Students Association* v. *Pacific Telephone and Telegraph Co.*, thought it compelling:

> Indeed the subject of the rights of homo-
> sexuals incites heated political debate today
> and the "gay liberation movement" encour-
> ages its homosexual members to attempt to
> convince other members of society that
> homosexuals should be accorded the same
> fundamental rights as heterosexuals. The aim
> of the struggle for homosexual rights, and
> the tactics employed, bear a close analogy to
> the continuing struggle for civil rights waged
> by blacks, women and other minorities.[5]

Some commentators sensitive to civil liberties found the decision full of "stirring language" and "heart-ening."[6]

These laudatory comments notwithstanding, the analogy between groups defined by race or sex, religious conviction, or national origin, and those who practice particular forms of behavior which are, as often as not, criminal[7] is not self-evident.

Close enough, say homosexuals about the distended analogy. But to make the analogy work requires covering up the distinctions between racial status and homosexual behavior. Many states make sodomy a crime, and these statutes have ancient roots. Sodomy was a criminal offense of common law and was forbidden by the laws of all the thirteen original states at the time the Bill of Rights was ratified. Although such statutes are now largely unenforced except in special circumstances (rape, child molestation, or various plea bargain compromises), it is hard to conceive how a group can achieve social acceptance of what they do when society has already decided to make what they do criminal and punishable by imprisonment.

Given this legal dilemma, homosexuals have sought through political or judicial means to have these laws invalidated, and in some states they have succeeded. Those efforts proved ultimately unavailing before the federal courts, however, when the Supreme Court ruled in *Bowers* v. *Hardwick* that a state law prohibiting consensual sodomy was constitutional.[8]

Homosexuals also sought refuge in a "right to privacy,"[9] the equal protection clause,[10] and various other theories attacking employment discrimination.[11] Since none of these refuges provided much protection, homosexuals adopted the more viable strategy of avoiding that legal thicket altogether. Instead, using to full effect the emotional power of appeals for rights and against discrimination, homosexuals began to propose ordinances that forbid discrimination in housing, employment, and public accommodations based on a person's "affectional or sexual preference" or "affectional or sexual orientation."

The fifty or so local ordinances on gay rights (nearly one-quarter of which are for municipalities in California) have varying provisions. They prohibit discrimination in public employment, public accommodations, private employment, housing and real estate, or in access to city facilities, services, and education. They may have affirmative action features, make violations criminal, and permit an aggrieved person to petition for injunctive relief. Some cities permit the award of damages, and some a reasonable attorney's fee. The ordinances also, depending on the political coalescence of forces necessary to pass them, may exempt landlord-owned or -occupied structures or religious institutions.

ANALYSIS OF HOMOSEXUAL CLAIMS: THE RATIONALE OF GAY RIGHTS EXPLORED

The real issue underlying the gay rights controversy is whether the law should give special protection for homosexual behavior. Does the inclination to practice anal or oral sodomy (or related sexual practices) with members of the same sex merit special legal safeguards?

The public policy issue is straightforward. A group of citizens, bound together by common sexual taste, comes seeking insulation of their sexual behavior from scrutiny by other members of society; they want, in short, to debar others from taking sexual orientation or behavior into account in making social decisions. They seek the privilege of having one aspect of their personality or behavior eliminated as a criterion for exercising a general right to associate, or dissociate, with others.

It is important that the issue be correctly stated. Much of the discourse about such political claims leaves underlying presuppositions unanalyzed. Among them is the presupposition that everyone has a preexisting right to protect his preferences and predispositions from being taken into account by other people. Referring to "gay rights" as "civil rights" is begging the question. It assumes such rights exist. With that assumption in place, the only question that remains is, have those rights been infringed? Has there been discrimination? Once discrimination has been shown, it follows that wrong should give rise to remedy. The remedy is explicit civil rights protections for homosexuals.

That model is defective. Civil rights protections have always required a sensitive balancing of social interests. On the one hand, a substantial social benefit is derived in continuing the historic deference given to human choices and discretion. The freedom of association valued by all Americans includes a corollary right to nonassociation. On the other hand, there is also a strong social benefit in discouraging arbitrary decisions that cause widespread injury to innocent parties. Human rights laws have struck a delicate balance that accommodates both interests. They give substantial relief to those who have been the victims of prejudice, but they do so without limiting the right of anyone to make decisions based on any reasonable criteria. By forbidding arbitrary or irrational decisions that cause substantial harm to innocent parties, human rights laws preserve intact discretionary decision making based on reason and common sense.

Looked at in an alternative way, homosexuals have all the same rights heterosexuals do. They are protected by the Bill of Rights,[12] by federal and state statutes[13], and by common-law decisions.[14] They have the same status before the law as do other citizens. Yet through gay rights ordinances, they demand to join the few classes of citizens having characteristics immune from scrutiny. The issue is not whether rights have been infringed. The issue is whether new rights, not previously recognized, should be created.

ARE GAY RIGHTS LAWS NECESSARY?

The legislative history of gay rights ordinances is typically long on emotion and short on evidence. There are no rigorous studies, and no substantial testimony, that prove homosexuals are routinely discriminated against. The legislative history underlying past battles over civil rights was filled with evidence that blacks suffered systematic discrimination against them in the South and structural forms of deprivation, such as isolation, in the North. Disparities in income, housing, employment, cultural opportunities, and education were not merely suspected, they were demonstrated by statistics, sociological studies, and voluminous testimony.

Lack of such proof here is no accident. As one observer has pointed out, "One of the most striking phenomena of the past few years is what appears to be a massive increase in the acceptability of homosexual behavior in America."[15] Aside from social pressure on those flaunting personality traits that would make heterosexuals equally unpopular, people do not routinely discriminate against homosexuals. Homosexuals live in nice neighborhoods, in well-furnished homes and apartments with expensive accouterments. They are popular in athletics (Billy Jean King, Martina Navratilova), in the arts (Rock Hudson, Boy George, Liberace, Truman Capote, and a long list of others), in Congress (Congressman Barney Frank), and in the professions.[16]

Indeed, homosexuals have become so strong in the marketplace that nearly every major manufacturer of consumer goods has a marketing plan directed specifically to them. Homosexuals have become a new "power bloc" that has both "votes and money."[17] One writer estimated that homosexuals control one-third of the buying power in California.[18] The estimate is inflated, but there is no doubt about homosexual influence. One wealthy New York homosexual estimated that homosexuals annually control as much as twenty billion dollars in New York City alone.[19] *Blueboy* magazine, a *Playboy*-style publication for homosexuals, found that its readers fit a classically middle-class profile. One homosexual has said that the "dominant style of New York . . . is set by visible homosexuals."[20]

This is exactly what an economist would anticipate in a free-market economy. When people have to pay a significant price to discriminate, they generally don't discriminate.[21] The homosexual does not need special privileges. They have become unnecessary.

Gay rights laws are also unnecessary when one considers the extensive rights the homosexual already has under existing law.[22] These rights supplement the routine constitutional privileges the homosexual has in common with all Americans: the Bill of Rights' protections, encompassing such things as freedom of speech, association, religious practice, due process of law; enforcement of contracts; use of the courts; equal protection of the law. In addition to such protections of law shared with all citizens, a homosexual can

- form organizations to lobby for his political rights.

- incorporate under state incorporation laws.

- form student organizations on state-supported campuses, including rights to the same benefits received by any other campus organizations, such as organized social functions and homosexual dances on campus.

- obtain tax-exempt and tax-deductible status.

- publicly assemble, rally, petition, and carry

out all forms of political activism in support
of his political ideas.

- wear badges and buttons in public schools
and colleges without fear of disciplinary
action by the school.

- force a public high school principal to allow
him to take a male to the school prom as a date.

- compel television and radio stations to
include members of the homosexual community in determining "community needs."

- be employed under the Civil Service. The
Civil Service Commission has given the
following directive to its supervisors: "You
may not find the person unsuitable for
Federal employment merely because that
person is a homosexual or has engaged in
homosexual acts."

This litany of rights is by no means exhaustive.
The homosexual has all the rights the heterosexual
does, but he wants a right the heterosexual does not
have. He wants to coerce others not to take into account
his inclination to practice sodomy, his prevailing
preference, even when those others, including parents,
employers, or landlords, have contrary convictions. The
result expands the privileges given to homosexuals and
shrinks the rights of other citizens.

The homosexuals' failure to demonstrate a need
for civil rights protections suggests that the true
agenda for their activism is not to rectify a limited list
of social grievances based on historic rights. Instead
they want public acknowledgment that the
homosexual lifestyle is as valid and upright as that of
the heterosexual and that they are entitled to the same

deference as blacks, religious groups, or women. One brochure put out by the Minnesota Committee for Gay and Lesbian Rights talks about the violation of "the most basic right—respect as people."[23] They want respect and acceptance of their behavior, an acceptance that is good neither for them nor for society.

One prominent psychiatric expert in the treatment of homosexuals is Dr. Charles Socarides, whose textbook on homosexuality is widely used in medical schools and who has written a number of journal articles on the treatment of homosexuals. Dr. Socarides believes that widespread acceptance of homosexuality is the worst thing that could happen to homosexuals since it ignores something the homosexual knows better than anyone else—that his actions are perverted and abnormal and require treatment. This is a terrible injustice for the homosexual, according to Socarides, and impairs our communal health.[24]

ARE GAY RIGHTS LAWS DESIRABLE?

Even if homosexuals believe gay rights laws are necessary, such laws would still be undesirable for society as a whole, for a number of reasons.

Gay Rights Laws Are an Inappropriate Addition to Human Rights Laws

As we have already seen, proponents of gay rights laws rely heavily on an analogy to other human rights legislation. If human rights laws have provided protection to other minorities, why should society not add one more group to those protected from discrimination? Hitching their wagon to the broadly based support Americans have traditionally given civil rights laws, gay rights advocates have made surprising progress in the past decade.

The human rights analogy, though popular and politically understandable, cannot withstand careful analysis. Adding homosexual behavior to a list of classes that includes racial and religious minorities makes no sense. The tenuous balance of social interests represented by these laws is reflected in the few, and carefully chosen, classes they protect. Relief has been given only in extraordinary circumstances. To add another protected class, at least five requirements have had to be shown: *(1)A demonstrable pattern of discrimination (2)based on criteria that are arbitrary and irrational (3)causing substantial injury (4)to a class of people with an unchangeable or immutable status (5)which has no element of moral fault.* Each of these requirements needs to be examined in some detail.

1. A demonstrable pattern of discrimination. The discrimination alleged must be more than a collection of isolated instances. There must be a clear pattern. At some time or other, everyone has been a victim of discrimination. A nervous applicant has lost a job opportunity because someone didn't like his tie or handshake or hairstyle. The beef-eater has been snubbed by the animal rights militant; the vegetarian has suffered the insults of the red-meat enthusiast. Everyone has an anecdote of some opportunity lost unfairly. The coercive power of law will only intervene, however, where there is a pervasive practice of discrimination throughout society. As was shown in the previous section, however, evidence of such a pattern of discrimination against homosexuals is almost totally lacking.

2. Based on criteria that are arbitrary and irrational. Civil rights laws do not limit anyone's freedom to make rational choices. They simply cancel a license to be prejudiced and to indulge irrational whims. Suppose a supervisor has been given the responsibility of hiring an employee for a day-care center. Who will be a better employee, a person whose skin is pigmented black, brown, white, yellow, or red? Would it be preferable to choose a Methodist over a Presbyterian? Is a Swiss a better diaper-changer than an Austrian? If one chooses to answer such silly questions at all, the only reasonable response would be, "It depends." It depends, of course, on the character of the individual. The status—black, Presbyterian, Swiss—is of no consequence to the rational decision-maker.

Arbitrariness is not a sufficient reason to prohibit the use of a particular criterion. Everyone makes hundreds of decisions a day which might not be rational, if all the facts were known. Human decision making is a complex calculus. Anyone who has served on a recruiting committee for his company knows that to be true. Both the objective and subjective data about an applicant are wildly variegated when seen through the prism of individual perceptions. Applicants are occasionally denied employment as a result of personality or a mannerism which may, in the long run, have no rational connection to the job the applicant was seeking.

When it comes to making choices among people, however, deviant sexual behavior tells significantly more about a person's character, or at least his characteristics, than does race, color, or religion. Even when done consensually and in private, homosexual behavior has spillover effects with public dimensions because it is a self-destructive, disproportionately disease-ridden behavior.[25]

Taking into account a person's perverted sexual orientation is neither arbitrary nor irrational. If the operator of a day-care center knows that a homosexual applicant statistically is a significant health risk, that he is peculiarly susceptible to infections especially dangerous for young children, that his promiscuity makes him anything but an appropriate role model for the children, is it socially responsible to make it illegal to take such relevant factors into consideration? Already some doctors are calling for more discriminating standards on who can give blood or work as food handlers or care for the physically weak—all as a result of shocking discoveries of homosexual health hazards. Is the law prepared to coerce people into ignoring facts that their common sense, moral convictions, and increasing medical knowledge tell them are relevant? If so, there may emerge a disrespect for the very laws in which many deserving minority groups have found refuge.

3. *Causing substantial injury.* Another element is whether or not there has been a demonstrable pattern of discrimination resulting in substantial injury. Public policy suggests that the creation of far-reaching rights ought not to be done in the absence of extensive wrongs and injuries. A substantial rationale for civil rights protection for blacks was, of course, a century of disproportionate access to wealth and other social benefits. Economists might differ on the reasons for this disproportionate sharing in social benefits, but the fact of disparate social status was clear.

Living with human beings in an imperfect world requires mutual tolerance. Society does not want to encourage people to run to the courts with every complaint, to guard tender egos from every slight, to seek damages for every insult. Laws give protection where the damage is demonstrably substantial. As the arguments of the previous section make clear, no such damage to homosexuals has been demonstrated.

4. To a class of people with an unchangeable or immutable status. Since the prophet Jeremiah observed that the Ethiopian could not change his color nor a leopard his spots, no one has questioned that everyone has, from the moment of birth, certain unchangeable features. Race, color, and national origin never change. The curious case of transsexuals notwithstanding, the same is true of sex. Each is what the law calls "an immutable characteristic." Although a person's religion may be for some a family inheritance and for others a personal decision, in neither case is it generally considered a whimsical preference. It is—if it means anything worthwhile—a set of deeply rooted, unchanging convictions that to the true believer is as unchangeable as his race, and that he has decided to embrace no matter the cost. At the very least, it is an expression of a long-recognized entitlement to have an opinion and express it. Aside from gay rights laws, no human rights law protects behavior. Certainly none protects preferences.

Some have perceived the homosexuals' claim that they have an immutable nature, a fixed orientation that draws them to commit sodomy with each other, as an important rationale for the creation of gay rights laws.[26] The key element is volition. If homosexuals cannot help being what they are, their argument for special protection in public accommodations and distribution of other social benefits seems more analogous to other civil rights claims.

Although immutability is one reason for special civil rights privileges, it alone is not a sufficient reason to give such protections. Many characteristics are immutable but not protected. The Sermon on the Mount asks, "Who of you by worrying can add a single cubit to his height?" Height is, at least without radical surgery, immutable, but height (or lack of it) is not protected. Biology suggests that an additional chromosome may predispose people to criminal conduct. That formation of chromosomes is immutable, but the class of persons committing sociopathic behavior is not protected. Even without embracing Skinnerian determinism one can believe that a great number of qualities and dispositions of people are largely immutable: good looks, mannerisms, predisposition to fat. Many of them are also criteria for important decisions. Jobs frequently go to those who are the nicest looking, the tallest, or have the most pleasing personalities, even though those qualities are essentially immutable characteristics. And few would dispute that it is appropriate to discriminate in hiring on the basis of ability.[27]

Even if immutability were a sufficient reason, those who advance gay rights measures ignore substantial evidence that homosexual behavior is not innate or immutable. As we discovered in the previous chapter, most psychiatrists view the innate or genetic explanation of homosexual behavior as a "myth" or "fallacy."[28] If homosexual behavior is not innate, it is therefore learned or acquired. It is not, as Dr. Socarides points out, "inevitable."[29]

5. Which has no element of moral fault. Human rights laws were never intended to give a social blessing to immorality. The classes they protect are all morally neutral. No moral fault is attached to being black or white, a native or an immigrant, a male or a female. The moral innocence of the victim of discrimination has made the need for such laws compelling. On the other hand, the inveterate liar, the flagrantly unfaithful husband, and the dishonest merchant should not be surprised at the social stigma their behavior produces.

If some people prefer not to associate with a compulsive womanizer who boasts, tiringly, of his amorous conquests, it is little wonder that they are not keen to associate with the average homosexual who has ten times as many partners as the most voracious heterosexual. Part of the wisdom of the human rights laws is to focus only on groups that all agree are morally neutral; without such a focus, social support for such legislation could crumble.

Gay rights laws are occasionally supported by an ideological twist on these facts.[30] Some argue that these laws are necessary to prevent a moral hegemony from interfering with our pluralistic society, and that homophobia stands in the way of full equality. Those who advocate conventional morality will necessarily frustrate the legitimate aspirations of a minority whose moral views differ. Homosexuality, by this standard, is simply an "alternative life-style" of equal morality and propriety with heterosexual behavior. Recognizing its legitimacy subverts the "establishment" of narrow, sectarian morality.

Such an argument is equally sectarian. One can construct a philosophical system which affirms the morality of all forms of sexual expression, including incest, bestiality, necrophilia, transvestism, or exposure. To a person with this philosophical inclination, it is unfair or unreasonable to discriminate on the basis of which particular form of sexual expression one chooses. But such a relativistic moral scheme is not shared by all. Some might consider homosexual sodomy legitimate under certain circumstances but shrink at bestiality—or believe the converse. A narrow slice of society might see nothing wrong with consensual sexual activity with minors; most abhor it.

Such divisions are to be expected in a pluralistic society and reflect the reason the analogy between homosexual behavior and genetic status breaks down. Character ought to be a relevant criterion. Because it ought to be a relevant criterion, people will assess character differently in a free society. No one can seriously argue that there is moral fault in being black or female, German or Chinese. But as the Supreme Court has recently stated, "To hold that the act of homosexual sodomy is somehow protected as a fundamental right would be to cast aside millennia of moral teaching."[31] To prohibit the use of such a criterion is, therefore, to take away a fundamental right of association, based on a good faith perception of moral character.

In short, gay rights laws meet none of the traditional requirements for human rights protection. Homosexuals have never been able to demonstrate a convincing pattern of discrimination that causes them substantial socioeconomic injury. They are a class of people linked together through behavior, not unchangeable status. Their actions are not morally neutral. Reasonable people—for reasons of deep-seated moral conviction, of health, of psychological stability, or of common sense—may wish to take a person's homosexual life-style into account in their decision making, all without the slightest tinge of bigotry or irrationality.

Gay Rights Laws Are a Door-opener to More Radical Steps

The lack of any compelling necessity and the homosexuals' attempt to squeeze into an ill-fitting niche (oppressed minority group) suggest that gay rights laws are not the objective, but are simply a way station en route to what homosexuals really want: full social acceptance. A review of homosexual demands, such as the following planks from the 1972 Gay Rights Platform,[32] reveals the accuracy of this assessment:

Federal:

- Amend all federal Civil Rights Acts, other legislation, and government controls to prohibit discrimination in employment, housing, public accommodations, and public services.

- Issuance by the President of an executive order prohibiting the military from excluding for reasons of their sexual orientation, persons who . . . desire entrance into the Armed Services; and from issuing less-than-fully-honorable discharges for homosexuality; and the upgrading to fully honorable all such discharges previously issued, with retroactive benefits.

- Federal encouragement and support for sex education courses, prepared and taught by Gay women and men, presenting homosexuality as a valid, healthy preference and lifestyle as a viable alternative to heterosexuality.

- Federal funding of aid programs of Gay men's and women's organizations designed to alleviate the problems encountered by Gay women and men which are engendered by an oppressive sexist society.

- Immediate release of all Gay women and men now incarcerated . . . because of sexual offense charges related to victimless crimes or sexual orientation; and that adequate compensation be made for the physical and mental duress encountered; and that all existing records relating to the incarceration be immediately expunged.

State:

- Repeal of all state laws prohibiting private sexual acts involving consenting persons; equalization for homosexuals and heterosexuals for the enforcement of all laws.

- Repeal of all state laws prohibiting solicitation for private voluntary sexual liaisons; and laws prohibiting prostitution, both male and female.

- Enactment of legislation so that child custody, adoption, visitation rights, foster parenting, and the like shall not be denied because of sexual orientation or marital status.

- Repeal of all laws governing the age of sexual consent.

- Repeal of all legislative provisions that restrict the sex or number of persons entering into a marriage unit; and the extension of legal benefits to all persons who cohabit regardless of sex or numbers.

If gay rights are granted, what will logically follow in these areas?

Education. Homosexual teachers in New York City have come out in support of the right of a teacher to have sex with a boy so long as it occurs outside the school.[33] The Gay Teachers Association has called for "A Bill of Rights for Gay Teachers and Students,"[34] which makes the following demands:

A BILL OF RIGHTS FOR
GAY TEACHERS AND STUDENTS

We, the members of the Gay Teachers Association, proud of our gay heritage and life-style, and believing strongly in the principles of free speech, the right to life, liberty, and the pursuit of happiness, and in the duty of gay people to strike out against bigotry and ignorance on every level, do herein:

Affirm our civil rights so that our right to work is insured

Affirm the beauty and legitimacy of our life style

Affirm the role of gay educators throughout history

Affirm our rights to educate all people about the outstanding contributions of gay writers, gay painters, gay historians, gay psychologists, sociologists, philosophers, and a host of other gay people who have invested their talents in the culture of a world society

Affirm the rights of gay students to non-judgmental information and counseling

Affirm that gay is proud

And in so affirming we set forth the following demands:

We demand that the board of education include in the preamble of its contract with our union the phrase "sexual orientation" in its listing of non-discriminatory practices

We demand that our union and all its affiliates work actively to see to it that this phrase be included in our contract

We demand that the principle of academic freedom be supported for gay teachers so that they need not fear affirming their sexual preference nor fear correcting misinformation which might occur in or out of the classroom

We demand all these things so that the cycle of oppression of gay people, oppression which stifles creativity, which stifles positive self-images can be terminated.

In a paper called "Lesbians and the Schools," Jean O'Leary, a prominent lesbian appointed by Jimmy Carter to the National Commission for the Observance of International Women's Year, demands that schools offer sex education courses "to encourage students to explore alternative lifestyles, including lesbianism," that school libraries be stocked with books extolling homosexuals, that homosexual clubs be established in schools to foster a community spirit among homosexuals, and that books that disparage homosexuality be banned. In addition, she recommends that students be furnished with names of homosexual counseling services available in the community and that teachers of "human sexuality courses" take a "positive view" of homosexuality.[35]

Affirmative action. The move for gay rights also bears with it the possibility of increasing demands for affirmative action, using the successes of the civil rights movement generally as a model. Already, homosexual activists have sought quotas in certain areas. The task force on the status of lesbian and gay male psychologists of the American Psychological Association, for example, demanded that "all panels on homosexuality (at national and regional meetings) shall include at least one member of the Association of Gay Psychologists as a panel member, and all paper sessions (at national and regional meetings) shall include at least one member of the Association of Gay Psychologists to serve as a discussant."[36]

Repeal of sodomy laws. One long-term goal of the homosexual movement has been to repeal laws prohibiting sodomy. Although gay rights activists have concentrated on promoting gay rights ordinances, they have not abandoned their attack on existing sodomy statutes. As long as their behavior remains criminal, it is hard for them to argue that they deserve special protection for it. When challenging sodomy statutes, homosexuals argue that there is a "right to privacy" in the Constitution that protects private acts of consensual sodomy.

In making that argument, homosexuals rely on cases that interpret the Constitution as forbidding government interference with private decisions. And so, for example, a consensual "right of privacy" has been held to protect decisions about education and child-rearing, marriage, and more recently contraception and abortion.[37] Homosexuals have argued from these cases that just as the law cannot unconditionally forbid a couple to use birth control, it cannot forbid two consenting adults to commit sodomy in the privacy of a bedroom.[38]

Although homosexuals had some initial success in state and federal courts using such arguments, the Supreme Court settled the question in *Bowers* v. *Hardwick* (1986).[39] Mr. Hardwick had brought suit in federal district court, challenging the constitutionality of the Georgia statute that criminalized consensual sodomy. He lost at the district court level, but won on appeal to the Court of Appeals, which held that the Georgia statute violated his fundamental rights. The Supreme Court disagreed. In a vigorously written opinion, Justice White pointed out that any fundamental liberties protected by a right to privacy must be "implicit in the concept of ordered liberty," or deeply rooted "in the nation's history and tradition." Because sodomy was traditionally a criminal offense in all states, to find that a right to engage in anal or oral sodomy was deeply rooted in this nation's history and tradition or is "implicit in the concept of ordered liberty" would be "at best facetious." Summing up, the Court said:

> And if Respondent's submission is limited to the voluntary sexual conduct between consenting adults, it would be difficult, except by fiat, to limit the claimed right to homosexual conduct while leaving exposed to prosecution adultery, incest and other

sexual crimes, even though they are committed in the home. We are unwilling to start down that road.[40]

In a concurring opinion, Justice Burger pointed out the moral dimension:

To hold that the act of homosexual sodomy is somehow protected as a fundamental right would be to cast aside millennia of moral teaching.[41]

Justice Burger's opinion paralleled a recent circuit court decision from the District of Columbia Court of Appeals which had approved the discharge of a homosexual from the military. Finding homosexuality "a form of behavior never before protected and indeed traditionally condemned," that court held that its decision should be based on constitutional principle, not on shifting public opinion.[42] Such federal decisions have left homosexuals two options: convince state courts that there is a right to commit sodomy under the state constitution, or convince legislators to repeal the statute.

Because homosexual activists have been unable to convince the courts that their sexually deviant behavior should be given special protection, they have tried to work harder on Congress, state legislatures, and city councils. The passage of gay rights laws would inevitably lead to the repeal of sodomy laws.

Homosexual marriage. A recent priority is to give homosexual partnerships the same benefits given to heterosexual marriage. By explicit social policy, married couples receive significant legal benefits. They can file joint tax returns, inherit property, use gift and estate tax mechanisms to maximize their estate, bring wrongful death actions on behalf of a spouse, and enjoy a host of other benefits. Homosexuals want the same benefits for their frequently transitory relationships.[43] Several jurisdictions are considering domestic partnership legislation. Indeed, the Court of Appeals for the State of New York held in 1989 that a "domestic partnership" of two male homosexuals was the equivalent of marriage. The historic concept of marriage could be stretched to include homosexuals because the idea of marriage itself the court found to be a legal fiction. Gay rights laws can be used as a foot in the door to such social experimentation. If discrimination against homosexuals is wrong, why not let them marry?

Indeed, a major thrust of the homosexual rights movement will increasingly be to validate homosexual marriage. It is the final legitimation of homosexual behavior. "Homosexual marriage" is, or course, an oxymoron. It is a contradiction that makes no sense, lexically or legally. The word *marriage* itself means "the institution whereby men and women are joined in a special kind of social and legal dependence, for the purpose of founding and maintaining a family" (*Webster's New International Dictionary*). Homosexual relationships stretch this definition beyond recognition.

Legally, homosexual marriage is also a confusion. As Justice Harlan pointed out nearly thirty years ago, "the intimacy of husband and wife [unlike relations based on homosexuality, fornication, and incest] is necessarily an essential and accepted feature of the institution of marriage." Justice Harlan's position, nearly identical to that expressed by Thomas Jefferson two centuries earlier, is well-taken. The harsh reality is that all forms of sexual expression are not equally normal. Simulating a family is not being a family.

In addition, while truly monogamous marriage is a relationship without venereal diseases and attendant spillover costs to society, abnormal sex translates into substantial public expense. And once the bright line of exclusivity attached to heterosexual marriage is crossed, where will society stop? Will special privileges be given to those who by reason of culture, inclination, or private choice seek sexual outlet in polygamy, incest, or communal groupings?

Demeaning homosexuality. A final proposal is to make illegal the demeaning of a sexual orientation. Several gay rights laws include provisions making it unlawful to "deride" or "denigrate" homosexual status. While these laws are explained as an effort to discourage the taunting of homosexuals, their application is more far-reaching and could include criminal penalties for ministers who express from the pulpit the view that homosexual acts are shameful. To the extent such laws merely proscribe "terroristic threats," they add nothing to laws already in existence that make such threats illegal regardless of the sexual orientation of the victim. But these ordinances go further. An ordinance before the Seattle City Council would have made it illegal to "discredit, demoralize, or belittle another person by words or conduct" based on sexual orientation.[44] Such hate-crime measures have been introduced in Congress. A Seattle prosecutor commented it would be a "new tool" in his arsenal. The tool is unfortunately so blunt that it could be used against those who "belittle" or "discredit" homosexuals by calling sodomy perverted or sinful. One Swedish pastor was sentenced to jail for preaching a sermon from Romans 1 that was found to be belittling to homosexuals. Interestingly enough, groups historically identified with free speech, such as the American Civil Liberties Union (ACLU), support laws that could restrict the freedom to express deeply rooted religious convictions. Gay rights laws are but a step on the way to such destinations.

Gay Rights Laws Use the Coercive Power of Law to Take Away Important Rights

While many focus on the alleged liberating effect of gay rights laws, few people focus on the coercive impact of such statutes. Violations of the gay rights provisions of a Duluth, Minnesota, human rights ordinance (passed over the mayor's veto and later overwhelmingly rescinded in a citizens' repeal effort) led to serious civil liability. Upon showing that a person had violated the ordinance, the court could, among other things, order the defendant to pay compensatory damages for mental anguish or mental suffering in an amount up to three times the amount for all such damages sustained. The reach of the ordinance was so broad that an employer could not have prevented an employee from coming to work "in drag" (wearing the clothes of the opposite sex) since to do so would be to punish a person for "projecting" his "sexual preference and identity."

The combination of a broadly worded ordinance and strong enforcement provisions is the stuff of which legal nightmares are made. Such ordinances give to homosexuals and take away from society at large. They take away, among other things:

- The right of parents or school districts to control the moral caliber of the person who teaches their children.

- The right of an employer to determine whether an applicant's moral character will affect his job performance.

- The right of churches and other religious

entities to exclude, or refuse to hire, someone whose life-style is contrary to their religious convictions.

Most of the proposed gay rights ordinances technically provide legal protection for more than just homosexuals. They typically provide protection to anyone, regardless of sexual preferences. A literal-minded judge would find that such laws give protection to a large number of sex criminals. Take, for example, the possible protected behaviors under a gay rights ordinance in Alexandria, Virginia:

- A convicted child molester, homosexual or heterosexual, could sue a day-care center that refuses to hire him, claiming discrimination on the basis of his "sexual orientation"; such an ordinance would thus protect behavior declared criminal under state law.

- A motel owner could be sued if he refused to rent a room to an unmarried couple. This would be discrimination in the use of "public accommodations." This would also be discrimination on the basis of "sexual orientation," in this case their sexual preference for unmarried people or for people married to someone else. Such an ordinance would contradict state public policy by protecting behavior declared criminal under state law.

- An insurance company could be sued for refusing to extend health insurance benefits to the sodomy partner of a homosexual or to the wives of a polygamist. The insurance company would be discriminating on the basis of "sexual orientation" by refusing to extend coverage to "spouses" because of their sexual preference. Since both sodomy and polygamy are prohibited under Virginia state law, such an ordinance would protect behavior already declared criminal.

- A landlord who refuses to rent or sell a facility to a person running a house of prostitution could be sued for refusing to rent or sell housing based on the person's "sexual orientation." Yet prostitution is a crime under Virginia law.

- A bank that refuses to loan money to a moviemaker who enjoys making and selling child pornography would be discriminating against the moviemaker on the basis of his "sexual orientation." Yet the making and selling of child pornography is a crime under most state laws.

- Law enforcement officials who arrest the customers of prostitutes, pornography stores, or child sex rings could be sued under the ordinance for "obstruction of practices unlawful under this chapter" if it is viewed that the police are discriminating against people who patronize certain "public accommodations" based on their specific "sexual orientation." Prostitution, the sale of pornography, and sex with children are all crimes under state statutes. Such an ordinance could protect behavior declared criminal under state law.

Those who think such results unlikely need only review the surprising interpretations courts give broadly worded laws.

Some, but not all, such ordinances contain an exemption for jobs where normal sexual practice might be a "bona fide occupational qualification" (BFOQ). But the applicability of a BFOQ, as civil rights laws prove out, is often dependent on the eye of the beholder. A pastoral position may be one permitting the assertion of a heterosexual BFOQ. But the organist, song leader, or Sunday school superintendent positions would most likely not be. And such exceptions are, in the interpretation of civil rights laws, narrowly construed.

Gay Rights Laws Will Coerce People to Violate Their Consciences

More compelling than the uncertain reach of such ordinances is their effect in coercing men and women of religious conviction to violate their consciences. Gay rights laws declare sexual preference to be amoral. As Dr. Jud Marmor has said, "Moral character is not determined by sexual preference, and individual homosexuals should be evaluated on their own merits and not on the basis of stereotyped behavior."[45]

But homosexual behavior is morally repugnant to a large number of people of varying religious traditions. Such laws might compel churches, religious schools, or other religious organizations to hire persons whose sexual practices contradict their religious doctrines; the laws could force these groups to adopt costly affirmative action programs to hire people who practice behavior they consider sinful. Such laws could force religious organizations that run shelters for battered women and the homeless, soup kitchens, or day-care centers to hire homosexuals in violation of church doctrine, or lose government funding of their operations.

Those who make judgments based on perceived moral character are placed in a hopeless predicament by such laws. The threat of legal sanctions presents such a person with no choice but to violate his conscience or violate the law.

Society Has Every Right to Prefer Heterosexual to Homosexual Behavior as a Matter of Social Policy

Society need not be ashamed of promoting the family. It can legitimately encourage people to organize themselves into families in order to get special social privileges. Strong families are the foundation of a strong society. Through providing essential services to society such as procreation, education, character formation, and protection and provision for young and old, the family renders incalculable benefits that society can reasonably reward.

The U.S. Supreme Court has recognized the centrality of the family. In an opinion on the right of privacy, Justice Harlan said:

> The right of privacy most manifestly is not an absolute. Thus, I would not suggest that adultery, homosexuality, fornication and incest are immune from criminal enquiry, however privately practiced . . . but the intimacy of husband and wife is necessarily an essential and accepted feature of the institution of marriage, an institution which the State not only must allow, but which always and in every age it has fostered and protected.[46]

Homosexuality, on the contrary, is essentially antifamily. It encourages promiscuous sexuality, a self-centered morality, and socially irresponsible behavior that exacts huge costs from society. The law has every right to discourage people from entering into paths that are demonstrably destructive—physically and psychologically—first to themselves, then to society itself.

Social Acceptance Should Not Be Given to Immoral Behavior

Conventional wisdom tells us that to tolerate weakness is often a virtue; to encourage immorality is always a vice. Gay rights laws that give special protections and privileges to people who practice sexual perversion are little more than a reward for immorality.

Anyone who has dealt with exhibitionists knows the terrible shame they experience. Often from good families, wrestling with a strange compulsion they find almost impossible to control, they expose themselves in public libraries or on street corners, then appear in court too ashamed to talk about their escapades to court-appointed lawyers. It is one thing to feel compassion for them. It is quite another to join with them in a parade down Fifth Avenue to St. Patrick's Cathedral, dressed in raincoats and carrying placards celebrating "Flashers' Pride." All decent people applaud the Augustine who repents from his hedonistic life-style and lives a life of Christian purity. But a publicly celebrated "Adulterers' Pride Day" should be viewed with contempt.

Public officials nonetheless often rush to be identified with "Gay Pride." No one should take pride in his own immoral behavior, but is it not worse to encourage another to take pride in behavior that is destroying him?

Gay rights, therefore, pose a paradox for society. The creation of novel rights will inevitably create new wrongs: wrongs to religious institutions that seek to use their facilities or hire their employees in accordance with their historic beliefs; wrongs to society by proliferation of a now-accepted behavior that is demonstrably costly to society; wrongs to individuals injured directly or indirectly by homosexual behavior; wrongs to the family structure which is the chief building block of society. Civil rights statutes should continue to prohibit judgments based on color and true status, and to encourage judgments based on character.

Chapter 3, Notes

1. D. C. Code Ann. §§ 1-250 to 2557 (1981).
2. *Gay Rights Coalition of Georgetown University Law Center* v. *Georgetown University*, 536 A.2d 1 (D.C. 1987). The court did hold that the university did not have to recognize or "endorse" the homosexual group.
3. Chief Justice Stone apparently coined the phrase, saying that "prejudice against discrete and insular minorities may be a special condition, which tends seriously to curtail the operation of those political processes ordinarily relied upon to protect minorities, and which may call for correspondingly more searching judicial inquiry." *United States* v. *Carolene Prods*, 304 U.S. 144, 152 (N. 4 (1938).
4. "Developments in the Law: Sexual Orientation and the Law," *Harvard Law Review* 102 (1989):1508, 1668, n.51.
5. *Gay Law Students Association* v. *Pacific Telephone and Telegraph*, 24 Cal.3d 458, 488, 595 p2d. 592, 610, 156 Cal.Rptr. 14, 32 (1979).
6. See E. Boggan, M. Haft, C. Lister, J. Rupp, and T. Stoddard, *An ACLU Handbook: The Rights of Gay People*, rev. ed. (1983), 17.
7. States that have criminal sodomy laws are Alabama, Arizona, Arkansas, Florida, Georgia, Idaho, Kansas, Kentucky, Louisiana, Maryland, Massachusetts, Michigan, Minnesota, Mississippi, Missouri, Montana, Nevada, New York, North Carolina, Oklahoma, Pennsylvania, Rhode Island, South Carolina, Tennessee, Texas, Utah, and Virginia, and also the District of Columbia. Although most state sodomy statutes do not distinguish between homosexuals and heterosexuals, six states bar only homosexual acts of sodomy: Arkansas, Kansas, Kentucky, Missouri, Montana, and Nevada.
8. 478 U.S. 186 (1986). The Court said, "Precedent aside, however, Respondent would have us announce as the Court of Appeals did, a fundamental right to engage in homosexual

sodomy. This we are quite unwilling to do."

9. The law of privacy has not provided much solace for homosexuals. As one proponent of gay rights puts it, "The courts have refused, on non-existent grounds, to extend this right [of privacy] to homosexuals" (J. Baer, *Equality Under the Constitution* [Ithaca, N.Y.: Cornell University Press, 1983], 231). Courts have held, for example, that the right of privacy does not protect extramarital relationships. J. S. Mill's classic statement on privacy held that society shall not meddle with "purely personal conduct."

10. The Ninth Circuit has recently held that discrimination against homosexuals in the military violates the equal protection clause. The decision conflicts with other decisions and is unlikely to be followed by the Supreme Court. The Supreme Court has granted unequivocal suspect status to only three classes: race, national origin, and alienage. See *State* v. *Walsh* 713 SW.2d 508, 510 (Mo. 1986).

11. Various forms of disparate treatment of homosexuals have been permitted by the courts in employment situations. Flaunting a homosexual life-style has been held, for example, to justify government termination of employment See *Singer* v. *United States Civil Service Commission*, 530 F.2d 247 (9th Cir., 1976).

12. Some statutes authorizing dismissal of teachers for "immorality" have been found unconstitutionally vague. For example, see *Burton* v. *Cascade School District Union High School*, 353 F.Supp. 254 (D. Ore., 1973).

13. Homosexual behavior is not, of course, generally protected. Title VII of the Civil Rights Act of 1964 has been held, for example, not to protect homosexuals. See *DeSantis* v. *Pacific Tel. and Tel.*, 13 CCH EPD par. 11,335 (D. Cal., 1976).

14. Some states, for example, have allowed homosexuals to adopt their partner. Other courts differ. Some courts have not permitted those who simulate sexual roles to marry (*Baker* v. *Nelson*, 291 Minn. 310, 191 N.W.2d 185 [1971]) and, on occasion, have denied custody to homosexual parents (*Chaffin* v. *Frye*, 45 Cal. App.3rd 39, 119 Cal. Rptr. 22 [1975]).

15. E. Rueda, *The Homosexual Network* (Greenwich, Conn.: Devin-Adair Publishers, 1982).

16. H. Brown, *Familiar Faces, Hidden Lives: The Story of Homosexual Men in America Today* (Orlando, Fla.: Harcourt Brace Jovanovich, 1976).

17. Coleman, "Washington Gay Vote," *Washington Post*, 21 April 1979.

18. S. Steele, "Business Affairs," *The Voice*, 27 March 1981, 30; see generally Dennis Altman, *The Homosexualization of America* (Boston: Beacon Press, 1982), 18ff.

19. Rueda, *Homosexual Network*, 177.

20. Altman, *Homosexualization of America*, 33.

21. G. Becker, *The Economics of Discrimination* (Chicago: University of Chicago Press, 1963).

22. See Norman Dorsen, ed., *The Rights of Gay People* (first published as *The Basic ACLU Guide to a Gay Person's Rights*) (New York: Bantam Books, 1983). See generally, "Developments in the Law," 1508.

23. Minnesota Committee for Gay and Lesbian Rights, *Working for the Equal Rights of Lesbians and Gay Men* (pamphlet).

24. Charles Socarides, "Homosexuality: Basic Concepts and Psychodynamics," *International Journal of Psychiatry* 10 (1972):120.

25. Commentators in favor of gay rights generally ignore, or pass by lightly, the substantial evidence that homosexual behavior has damaging consequences, including enormous physical dangers, both to homosexuals and to public health. (See previous chapter.)

26. Support for the idea that acquisition of homosexuality is immutable because it is not subject to control (or develops early, then is fixed) is contained in the following: C. Warren, "Homosexuality and Stigma" in *Homosexual Behavior: A Modern Reappraisal*, ed. J. Marmor (New York: Basic Books, 1980), 125-26; R. Kronemeyer, *Overcoming Homosexuality* (New York: Macmillan, 1980), 195; C. Tripp, *The Homosexual Matrix* (New York: McGraw-Hill, 1975).

27. Tom Lehrer once called the U.S. Army the ultimate equal opportunity employer because it "did not discriminate on the grounds of race, creed, color . . . or ability."

28. "Neither present-day endocrinological tests nor microscopic or clinical examinations have revealed any physiological differences between a heterosexual and a homosexual." J. McCary, *Sexual Myths and Fallacies* (New York: Van Nostrand Reinhold, 1971), 94.

29. Socarides, "Homosexuality," 118. See also I. Bieber, *Homosexuality: A Psychoanalytic Study of the Male Homosexual* (New York: Basic Books, 1962).

30. For a pro-gay rights approach to sexual orientation law see Rivera, "Queer Law: Sexual Orientation Law in the Mid-80s," *University of Dayton Law Review* 11 (1986):275; Chatin and Lefcourt, "Is Gay Suspect?," *Lincoln Law Review* 8 (1973):24; Dressler, "Judicial Homophobia: Gay Rights Biggest Roadblock," *Civil Liberties Review* (Jan.-Feb. 1979):19, 22. See also Revere, "Our Strait-laced Judges: The Legal Position of Homosexual Persons in the United States," *Hastings Law Journal* 30 (1979):799.

31. *Bowers* v. *Hardwick*, 478 U.S. 186, 106 S.Ct. 2841 at 2847 (1986). See also Romans 1:24-27; 1 Corinthians 6:9-11; Jude 7.

32. 1972 Gay Rights Platform, drawn up at the National Coalition of Gay Organizations convention, Chicago, 1972 (Rueda, *Homosexual Network*, 202-3).

33. "Gays in the Classroom," *New York Post*, 11 July 1979.

34. Gay Teachers Association, "A Bill of Rights for Gay Teachers and Students" (Albany, 1982).

35. O'Leary and Vida, "Lesbians and the Schools," paper circulated at the Nebraska International Women's Year Conference, Lincoln, 25-26 June 1979.

36. Rueda, *Homosexual Network*, 129. It is often a short step from equality to "preference."

37. *Griswold* v. *Connecticut* 381 U.S. 479 (1965) and *Roe* v. *Wade* 410 U.S. 1113 (1979).

38. See *Oklahoma City School Board* v. *National Gay Rights Task Force* 727 F.2d 1270 (10th Cir., 1984; U.S., 1985).

39. 478 U.S. 186 (1986).

40. Ibid.

41. Ibid.

42. The Supreme Court appeared to follow the reasoning of an earlier decision in the District of Columbia Court of Appeals, *Dronenburg* v. *Zech*, in which Judge Bork upheld the discharge of a U.S. Navy petty officer who had repeatedly engaged in sodomy with one of his recruits. See *Dronenburg* v. *Zech* 741 F.2d 1288 (D.C. Cir., 1984).

43. See "Same Sex Marriage and the Constitution," *Legal Problems and Family Law* (University of California, Davis *Law Review* 6 [1973]:275).

44. "Menacing Gays Could Be Made a Crime," *Seattle Post-Intelligencer*, 11 May 1984.

45. "Men and Boys: The Boston Conference," *Gaysweek*, 12 February 1979, 9.

46. *Poe* v. *Ullman* 367 U.S. 492, 522, n.3 (1961), J. Harlan dissenting.

Chapter Four

Gay Rights and Religion

Wherefore God also gave them up to uncleanness through the lusts of their own hearts, to dishonour their own bodies between themselves: who changed the truth of God into a lie, and worshipped and served the creature more than the Creator, who is blessed for ever. Amen.

For this cause God gave them up unto vile affections: for even their women did change the natural use into that which is against nature: and likewise also the men, leaving the natural use of the woman, burned in their lust one toward another; men with men working that which is unseemly, and receiving in themselves that recompence of their error which was meet.

And even as they did not like to retain God in their knowledge, God gave them over to a reprobate mind, to do those things which are not convenient (Romans 1:24-28).

Homosexual militants have long perceived another barrier to their objectives: traditional religious convictions that homosexual behavior is immoral. Just as the homosexual felt stigmatized when his sexual behavior was listed as a "mental disorder" by the psychiatric community, so he feels he cannot be accepted while there remain churches and individuals who believe his conduct is a sin. As a result, homosexuals have not overlooked the battlefield of theology in their campaign for legitimacy.

THE HOMOSEXUAL ATTACK ON TRADITIONAL MORALITY

Homosexuals recognize the political dimensions of theological controversies. If "guerrilla theater" and propaganda can influence scientists to repeal their findings, cannot the same tactics dilute accepted doctrine or forge new church teaching?

To that end, homosexuals began to demand that they be represented in any study done by church officers. The Roman Catholic homosexual group Dignity, for example, demanded of Baltimore's archbishop, William Borders, that the "gay and lesbian" community advise the archbishop on homosexuality.[1] They have sought systematically to make sure opposing voices within the church are not heard. A "gay activist alliance" convinced WOR-TV to edit out allegedly antihomosexual remarks made by evangelist James Robison on his weekly radio program.[2] They have applied substantial pressure on individual church bodies to alter their stance. The reason for the pressure is not difficult to discern.

There is no question that the main stumbling block in the theoretical and practical acceptance of homosexuality by American society has been traditional religion. This has been perfectly understood by the leadership of the homosexual movement.[3]

The traditional moral view has an ancient and diverse following. In 538 Emperor Justinian said:

Since certain men, seized by diabolical incitement, practice among themselves the most disgraceful lusts, and act contrary to nature: we enjoin them to take to heart the fear of God and the judgment to come, and to abstain from such like diabolical and unlawful lusts, so that they may not be visited by the just wrath of God on account of these impious acts, with the result that cities perish with all their inhabitants.[4]

Henry VIII removed cases of sodomy from the ecclesiastical courts and made them a capital crime, which he called "the detestable and abominable vice of buggery."[5] Sir Edward Coke wrote: "Buggery is a detestable and abominable sin, amongst Christians not to be named, committed by carnal knowledge against the ordinance of the creator and order of nature."[6] The great legal commentator Blackstone called homosexuality an act "the very mention of which is a disgrace to human nature."[7] Many polls have established that religious people view homosexuality as a sin, and that those who view it as a sin also overwhelmingly view it as abnormal.

Some, of course, have approached the matter with humor. Evelyn Waugh once said when asked why there are no good proofreaders left in England: "Because clergymen are no longer unfrocked for sodomy."[8]

But the homosexuals are deadly serious. In

mounting this attack, they have devised separate strategies for the different theological traditions. They correctly perceived that the "gay rights" approach would be the perfect vehicle to obtain acceptance from some church groups. The first to line up behind a gay rights agenda have been those churches and denominations characterized by liberal interpretation of the Bible, churches which do not acknowledge the authority and supremacy of the Bible. In one congressional hearing, for example, the Reverend Cecil Williams was asked whether there were "moral absolutes" which do not change. The Reverend Williams had long been pastor of the Glide Memorial Church in San Francisco, a church that had performed homosexual weddings and caused a major stir in the mid-seventies. Reverend Williams took the liberal view in answer to the question:

> There are no absolutes. All absolutes have to be looked at, criticized, reinterpreted, revised. That is why you have revised versions of the Bible. It is to reestablish, redirect, make relevant, the word in a different time and at a different condition and in different circumstances. That is merely one way of looking at it. There are no absolutes that should not and cannot be reinterpreted and redefined as well as to create different responses for the times during which people live.[9]

By such an interpretation, major social change causes, at least potentially, major theological change. Religion is the tail and common mores are the dog. Pastors reinterpret the Bible to bless a new sociological or political consensus. The church does not stand outside of culture, with an authoritative plumbline, but becomes a facilitator of moral revolution. Such churches quickly acknowledged gay rights efforts and occasionally authorized or participated in demonstrations against churches which preached a Bible-based view of sexuality. Gay rights planks were adopted by the National Council of Churches and the Union of American Hebrew Congregations, among others.

A second major religious tradition comprises those who acknowledge an authoritative standard. To some, as in the Roman Catholic tradition, that authority comes from the official pronouncements of the church, combining the Bible with church tradition, papal encyclicals, and the like. To others in the Reformed and Protestant traditions, it comes from the Bible itself. For both Roman Catholics and Evangelicals, homosexuality traditionally has been viewed as a grave evil.

For these churches, the homosexuals needed to take the religious tradition as a given, but reinterpret it to permit homosexual behavior. At a practical level, homosexuals have sought to penetrate these churches to make their suggested changes in theology more palatable.

Again, homosexuals resorted to the time-worn strategy. First came confrontation. At one major Roman Catholic conference, a "gay liberation front" group interrupted the proceedings to say:

We are homosexuals!

As members of the Gay Liberation Front, we deny your right to conduct this seminar.

It is precisely such institutions as the Catholic church and psychiatry which have created and perpetuated the immorality myth and stereotype of homosexuality which we as homosexuals have internalized, and from which we now intend to liberate ourselves.[10]

Along with these more confrontational approaches, there have been cooperative endeavors. The homosexual group Dignity sought out sympathetic priests to open churches for fundraisers, workshops, and various homosexual events. Such approaches sought the sympathy of the Roman Catholic church for homosexuals who wanted to remain in the church even while continuing their conduct. Gradually the position of many priests and intellectuals in the church began to erode. What used to be a clear case of serious moral disorder became more confusing. Today many of these churches actually fund homosexual causes. Finally, a prominent Jesuit magazine, *America*, could write:

> The use of Biblical injunctions against homosexuality by Anita Bryant and her followers was hopelessly fundamentalistic. Theological scholarship, whether scriptural or ethical, recognizes today that the application of scripture texts that condemn homosexuality is dubious at best. The phenomenon of homosexuality, as it is understood today, covers too wide a range of inclinations and behavior patterns to be subject to sweeping condemnations. Furthermore, the overall tone and principle argument of the "save our children" campaign not only lack[ed] Christian compassion toward homosexuals but also violated basic justice in perpetuating a lie.[11]

Other Roman Catholics, such as Charles Curran, began to accept the notion that homosexuals could not help themselves, saying, "Some people, through no fault of their own, are homosexual."[12] One Roman Catholic priest has documented carefully the overwhelming infiltration of the Roman Catholic church by the "homosexual network."[13]

The movement has also sought to influence those who look exclusively to the Bible for authority, an endeavor every bit as daunting as infiltration of the Roman Catholic church. But soon there began to appear books such as Ralph Blair's *An Evangelical Look at Homosexuality* and Scanzoni and Mollenkott's *Is the Homosexual My Neighbor? Another Christian View.* Suddenly, what had been clear for centuries was now becoming hazy.

THE BIBLICAL VIEW OF HOMOSEXUAL BEHAVIOR

On its face, the biblical view of homosexual behavior could not be clearer. It is, quite simply, an "abomination." Because men turn from God to worship humanistic inventions, God gives them up to unnatural lusts that devastate them, spiritually and physically. With the impatience of a schoolteacher repeating an elementary lesson, the apostle Paul counsels the Corinthians not to kid themselves: homosexual offenders will not inherit the kingdom of God unless they repent (1 Corinthians 6:9-10). Jude paints a picture worth a thousand words: the sulfurous barrenness of the south shore of the Dead Sea, the only residue of once-flourishing Sodom and Gomorrah, gives God's most dramatic statement on a sensate culture given to homosexuality (v. 7).

These are only a few of the numerous condemnations of sodomy in the Bible. Actually fifteen scriptural terms characterize or identify the sin of sodomy, including, among others, *abomination* (Leviticus 18:22), *lusts* (Romans 1:24), *wicked* (Genesis 13:13), *vile affections* (Romans 1:26), *against nature* (Romans 1:26), *unseemly* (Romans 1:27), *strange flesh* (Jude 7), *reprobate mind* (Romans 1:28). Homosexual prostitutes are called *dogs* (Deuteronomy 23:18).

Christianity is not alone in its assessment. Every major religious tradition views homosexuality as an egregious moral offense against a God who created human beings male and female and told them to "fill the earth." Most, if not all, primitive tribes have a taboo against homosexual behavior, reflecting what Paul says in his analysis of homosexuality in Romans 1: God's truth is perfectly plain in nature so that men are without excuse.

Because homosexuality is an offense against nature as well as against revealed religion, it is properly legislated against by lawmakers. There is no authority in the Bible for legislating faith in Jesus Christ or requiring acts of worship. That would make conversion meaningless. But laws against homosexual acts are not only permissible but embody one of the fundamental purposes of law. As Paul says in 1 Timothy 1:8-11, laws prohibiting homosexuality are genuine expressions of the purpose of law itself. Lumping homosexuality together with murder, slave trading, and other serious crimes, he says that the law "is not made for a righteous man, but for the lawless and disobedient."

THE REVISIONIST VIEW OF HOMOSEXUAL BEHAVIOR

No matter how plain the words, many theologians have "reexamined" the Bible on this subject and come up with some revisionist—indeed astonishing—conclusions. Like those who reexamine historical documents and find that Hitler was innocent, that Lee Harvey Oswald was railroaded, and that Alger Hiss was patriotic, those who believe that the "Bible nowhere condemns homosexuality" face a daunting assignment. There is some major explaining away to do. It is a familiar pattern: worldly culture leads the way (feminism, Marxism, homosexuality) and compliant theologians follow, explaining how "keep silent" means "speak," "do not steal" means "forcibly redistribute income," and "abomination" means "live and let live."

A variety of statements by religious groups reflect this trend. For example, one mainline denomination has addressed the topic in a brochure titled *Resources for Ministry*:

> Certainly the Bible does condemn lustful, exploitative and dehumanizing sexual behavior—both homosexual and hetero-sexual. However, nowhere are loving committed relationships between persons of the same gender condemned. . . . Today, gay Christians and their non-gay supporters affirm homosexuality as a gift of God to be celebrated just like the gift of heterosexual orientation.[14]

The "Social Justice Committee" of the Minnesota Council of Churches, an ecumenical body composed of most of the mainline denominations in the state, adopted a similar statement on homosexuality. It said in part,

> God's intended wholeness includes human sexuality as a gift for the expression of love and the generation of life. . . . There may be creative and whole expressions of one's

sexuality at various levels in relationships between men and women, between men and other men, and between women and other women. We seek to enable persons to understand and to act out their sexuality in ways which are life-giving to themselves and to other persons with whom they are in relationship.[15]

The statement goes on to condemn an attitude that views homosexuality as "something to hide or exorcise" rather than "something to celebrate." Homosexuals "are best understood as a 'people who have been sinned against.' "

Such views are not the exclusive province of liberal church groups. In *An Evangelical Look at Homosexuality*, Ralph Blair, a member of the National Association of Evangelicals, says,

Part of the task of evangelicals is to abandon unbiblical crusades against homosexuality and to help those who have quite naturally developed along homosexual lines to accept themselves as Christ accepted them—just as they are and to live lives which include responsible homosexual behavior.[16]

In *Sex for Christians*, Fuller Theological Seminary professor Lewis Smedes recommends "optimum homosexual morality," that is, a permanent, "non-exploitative" relationship between homosexuals who "can manage neither change nor celibacy."[17] In *The Sexual Revolution*, a Dutch pastor calls for evangelicals to develop a "viable homosexual ethic" calling for "permanent relationships between unchangeable homosexuals."[18]

To say that homosexuals cannot be changed is uninformed. To say they will lovingly limit their perverted practices to one person is naive. But to say that the Bible approves of all this is incredible without a further understanding of the revisionist analysis. Even then it is by no means persuasive. The revised view has several themes:

The sin of Sodom and Gomorrah was inhospitality. The real offense that triggered the fire and brimstone was inhospitality.[19] Some go further and say that those who do not receive practicing homosexuals for ministry in the church are guilty of the sin of Sodom and Gomorrah, not the sodomites themselves.

It is true, to be sure, that those seeking to sodomize the heavenly visitors were guilty of breaching the important code of hospitality in the ancient Near East. That breach of etiquette no doubt aggravated the offense. But to say that inhospitality was the essential sin of Sodom is equivalent to saying the essential offense of John Gacy, the Chicago contractor who invited scores of adolescents to his home, sodomized them, and buried them in his basement, was inhospitality. Sodom was inhospitable to the visitors, but the sin that buried them beneath the wrath of God was pride and sensuality illustrated by abominable sexual behavior.

The men of Sodom only wanted to "get to know" the angels. Some have tried to support the inhospitality theory by arguing that the men of Sodom only wanted to become acquainted with Lot's visitors. Their disappointing and ultimately futile efforts to interrupt the social gathering caused God's judgment to fall.

The argument is linguistically untenable. Their intent was no different from that of the Benjamites in Judges 19:22-25, who settled for a woman only when there were no men available. The linguistic difficulties facing this revisionist view are compounded by the

New Testament's interpretation of why Sodom fell. According to Jude 7, Sodom fell because of "fornication and going after strange flesh." The idea that the men of Sodom had in mind a competitive tea party is not consistent with the Genesis account and its tone of sensual desperation.

The Bible condemns only homosexual behavior that is a part of pagan religious exercises. The abominable thing about men lying with men, the argument goes, is not the physical act. It is the connection of homosexual acts to male temple prostitutes, luring Jews to pagan worship condemned by God. Jews venturing into sexual acts with pagan prostitutes were surrendering their loyalty to the one God.

But Leviticus nowhere limits the prohibition on homosexual conduct to religious prostitution, any more than it limits the prohibition against bestiality to sex with beasts owned by foreigners. It simply forbids men lying with men (18:22).

The Bible only forbids homosexual activity by priests, and hence its prohibitions, like the ceremonial law, have disappeared. As a part of the Levitical law, some say, the regulations of Leviticus 18 are no longer in effect. They were for one group (priests) and one time (the old dispensation).

Such a view is wrong-headed. The rule in question was not for the priests alone. It is explicitly directed to the priests to teach the people. Moreover, biblical condemnations of homosexuality occur both before (Sodom) and after (the New Testament) the law. Those strong prohibitions make clear that homosexuality is a moral matter, going to the very core of creation and human sexuality.

New Testament condemnations of homosexuality

reflect cultural prejudice and don't address loving, committed homosexual relationships. The cultural argument is the final refuge of those who wish to avoid a clear command of the Bible. Scripture writers were limited by their upbringing and cultural milieu and such limitations make it necessary to disregard commands that manifest such cultural bias.

Such a view, if accepted generally, would eliminate the authority of the Bible entirely. Who is to say that the prohibition of adultery was not a cultural by-product of ancient biases before people discovered the benefits of "swinging"? Why not reason the same way for murder, theft (a pre-socialistic bias for private property?), or lying? In fact, sexuality and its physical expression are close to the core of Christian teaching. The ideal of Christian marriage exists from creation onward and takes its greatest nobility from its use as a model of the relationship between Christ and the church.[20] Commands to sexual purity saturate biblical ethics from Genesis to Revelation. Its counterpart, any sexual immorality outside of marriage, leads a number of lists of sins especially reprehensible.

THE DAMAGING CONSEQUENCES OF HOMOSEXUAL BEHAVIOR

Put simply, to those who believe that the Bible is the word of God, homosexuality is immoral because God says so. But even were there no explicit command in the Bible that forbade sodomy, it is easy to show that it is an unnatural act—whether by examining basic anatomy, hygiene, the physical and psychological consequences for the homosexuals themselves, the promiscuity and exploitation built into "normal" homosexual behavior, or by merely a head count of the world's religions. To ignore that reality, to pretend out of misguided compassion that homosexuals are to celebrate their sodomy, does incalculable moral damage.

To the extent such theology becomes embodied in law, it damages the social fabric. Most reasonable people reject the old nostrum that "you can't legislate morality." They realize that law is nothing but a statement of minimum public morality that teaches members of society a basic course in right and wrong. The law is society's "schoolmaster." The repeal of laws against sodomy, together with the creation of special homosexual privileges, teaches that homosexual behavior is a valid, alternative life-style and lures others to experiment with a destructive perversion.

It is also damaging to people seeking a moral compass. The Bible teaches that one of the most important building blocks of good character is to be able to discriminate between good and evil. This quality of discernment tells readers from whom one ought to take advice, with whom one ought to associate, to whom one ought to offer a job. The Christian ought to be able to recognize the adulteress, the fool, the covetous man, the mocker, the reprobate.[21] The erosion of moral boundaries threatens a fundamental and necessary part of Christian character: being able to separate the precious from the vile. Gay rights laws are the first antidiscrimination laws that prohibit Christians from making necessary moral judgments in forming important life decisions.

Finally, the revisionist theology is far from compassionate. It is cruel to homosexuals themselves. The sodomite is trapped in a lust that is destroying him by inches and yards. To tell him he cannot help himself, to tell him to rejoice in his fatal disease, is to consign him forever to unhappiness. Much better the simple message of Christian grace. You are a responsible moral being who has sinned grievously against God. God loves you but hates your life-style. You are headed for judgment, but there is a way out.

THE NEED FOR REPENTANCE

The Bible talks of *repentance*, a word that suggests to some modern minds the hair-shirted prophet bearing the solemn placard, "Repent!" It sounds like an antiquated concept, the stuff of Puritan caricatures.

But there is much sound theology in that single word. It suggests that there is a standard of right and wrong that does not change with changing mores. It suggests that those standards are as enduring as scientific laws which govern natural phenomena. Hidden within that word also is the idea that such standards are not only absolute, but good. When Moses gave his parting admonition to the nation of Israel, he told the people that he was setting before them life and death, blessings and cursings, and advised them to "choose life" (Deuteronomy 30:11-20). The moral law that God has established for his creatures is both good and life-giving; one departs from that standard at risk to his own life, health, and happiness.

Repent means, therefore, that a person must have a "change of mind" that brings his ideas into conformity with God's expressed directions for how to live a happy, healthy, and wholesome life. It means that one ought to repent not only as a sign of obedience to God and his will, but also for the good of his own life and future. It means also that he can repent, no matter how firm and unyielding the grip of sin and disorder may be on his life. A command given by a wise and good lawgiver implies the ability to comply with it.

The central religious question spiritually

searching people have always faced is, "How can a man be right with God?" The question arises out of our intuition that God is different from us. We are fallible, fumbling, feckless in our efforts to do right. He is wise, powerful, just. The answer to that question for Christians is to have a radical change of heart. When God's ways cross our ways, when his thoughts cross our thoughts, it is our imperative to change, to acknowledge our wrong, and to ask God's help to become right.

The formula the apostle Paul used in the public assembly and in his house-to-house visitation was, "Repentance toward God and faith in our Lord Jesus Christ." Repentance acknowledges the standard and our willingness to accept it. Faith in the Lord Jesus Christ means to acknowledge that he was God's anointed messenger from heaven who shared the human condition. Through his death and resurrection he was confirmed as Lord and life-giver who is willing to save and sanctify those who acknowledge him. This mystery of conversion fills a person with new power to overcome both the penalty of sin and its power. "If any man be in Christ," the Bible says, "he is a new creature."[22]

That transformation is never easy. It is not easy for the homosexual. It is not easy for the glutton, the materialist, the adulterer, the thief, the proud man, or any other of us with our peculiar besetting sins. But it is possible.

For the true Christian, the homosexual is not a moral pariah to declaim against. He is like the lost sheep, the lost coin, or the lost son depicted in three of Jesus' parables (Luke 15). The Christian, while condemning the homosexual movement for its false ideology, looks—as Jesus did—at the individual. The homosexual is the lost sheep who unwittingly has wandered away from the flock and exposed himself to serious and destructive dangers. The Christian longs to seek him out and bring him back with rejoicing.

As pitiable as a lost sheep, the homosexual is precious as the lost silver coin. The Christian wants to be as diligent as the woman looking to restore that lost silver coin to the other nine on her bridal necklace. The homosexual is of great worth.

Finally, the homosexual has the potential of the lost son. The lost son, having wasted his inheritance through enormous prodigality, is reduced to eating filthy husks of corn with the swine. But in his father's eye, he can be washed clean, wear a new robe, put on shoes and a ring of acceptance. So the homosexual has the potential to be a pure and attractive picture of Christ's power. He has the potential that every sinner has to be right in the eyes of God. The Christian, therefore, must be like the waiting father, ready to accept and embrace the truly repentant homosexual.[23]

Chapter 4, Notes

1. E. Rueda, *The Homosexual Network* (Greenwich, Conn.: Devin-Adair Publishers, 1982), 129.

2. Ibid.

3. Ibid., 243.

4. See Bullough, "Challenges to Societal Attitudes toward Homosexuality in the Late 19th and Early 20th Centuries," *Social Science Quarterly* 58 (June 1977):37.

5. See Ivan Illich, "Disabling Professions" in *Disabling Professions*, Ivan Illich et al. (London: Marion Boyers Publishers, 1977).

6. Garret et al., *Homosexuality in the Western Christian Tradition* (London: Longmans, Green and Co. 1955), 73.

7. Ibid.

8. Rueda, *Homosexual Network*, 246.

9. Ibid.

10. Ibid., 248.

11. *America*, 25 June 1977, 558.

12. "Homosexuals in Religious Life," *The Tablet*, 26 December 1981, 19.

13. Rueda, *Homosexual Network*, chapters 6 and 7.

14. *Resources for Ministry*, Committee on Ministry to/with Gay and Lesbian Persons of the Minnesota Synod-Lutheran Church of America (undated).

15. "Statement on Homosexuality," Social Justice Committee, Minnesota Council of Churches (1982).

16. R. Blair, *An Evangelical Look at Homosexuality* (Homosexual Community Counseling Center, 1972). Blair's views, of course, are his own, and do not reflect the opinion of the National Association of Evangelicals.

17. Lewis Smedes, *Sex for Christians* (Grand Rapids: Wm. B. Eerdmans Publishing Co., 1976), 73.

18. J. Rinzema, *The Sexual Revolution* (Grand Rapids: Wm. B. Eerdmans Publishing Co., 1974).

19. For this and the other tenets of the revisionist view listed below, see generally C. Philpot, *The Gay Theology* (Plainfield, N.J.: Logos, 1977); Rinzema, *Sexual Revolution*.

20. Ephesians 5:22-33.

21. Psalm 1:1; Proverbs 2:16, 7:6-23, 9:6-7, 11:15, 20:4; Micah 2:2; Romans 1:28.

22. 2 Corinthians 5:17. See 1 Corinthians 6:11 for an application of this truth to the homosexual condition.

23. 2 Corinthians 5:16-21.

Chapter Five

The Myth of the Victimless Crime:
The Social Side of Homosexuality and Laws Prohibiting Sodomy

"No man is an island . . ."
John Donne

T he past few decades have seen the rise of an idea peculiarly well suited to the individualism of modern America and to a prevailing obsession shared by several successive "me" generations. It is the idea that some crimes have no victims and therefore are not society's business. The law should keep its nose out of people's affairs, the theory goes, unless harm is being done to someone else.

This theory, a favorite of the American Civil Liberties Union, makes a neat distinction between crimes with victims—robberies, murders, arson, fraud—and crimes without victims—prostitution, pornography, drug use, consensual sodomy. It asks society to accept any behavior even if morally repugnant unless there is clear evidence of victimization of others. The old idea that there is a public morality that gives many significant, although intangible, social benefits is rejected, as is the Christian view that the morality of society is the most important determinant in its success and progress. "Righteousness exalteth a nation," wrote Solomon, "but sin is a reproach to any people" (Proverbs 14:34). Many who reject individualism in economic matters, however, rush to embrace it in moral matters, believing that tolerance demands a hands-off attitude.

Like all political misconceptions (at least those that attract adherents), there is a germ of truth to this analysis. A free society requires tolerance of diverse ideas. That government is indeed best that governs least. A free country leaves room for the free play of individual choices and decisions. But the idea of the victimless crime overlooks two key ingredients in human relationships: the centrality of morality and the power of influence.

As Jesus taught in the Sermon on the Mount through the metaphor of salt and light, the most important factor in human progress is the moral one. A virtuous people is a free and prosperous people, a proposition recognized by such diverse thinkers as Washington, Hamilton, Madison, and Jefferson. Economists such as Max Weber recognized the "protestant work ethic" as a key factor in economic growth. Modern criminologists, such as Harvard's James Q. Wilson, recognize that moral training is the best antidote to crime. Historians such as Edward Gibbon agree on the principle cause of the collapse of the Roman Empire: moral rot. Good morals percolate through society and influence it toward good character, which in turn has an unmistakable impact on society at large. Bad morals work insidiously to cause decay. Christians believe that it is not the economic determinism of Marx, nor the sexual determinism of Freud, nor the evolutionary determinism of Darwin that best explains the meaning of history, but the moral determinism of the Bible. And that determinism spreads through society not by some kind of fiat, but by moral ideas.

Science recognizes the power of influence. A pebble dropped in the lake sends waves that lap to the farthest shore. Even more significant is the influence of complex interrelationships among men. "None of us liveth to himself," Paul says (Romans 14:7). The Bible teaches that all men have the same nature. We are all members of one organic whole. And our bond of physical relationship is strengthened by the universal interdependence of men upon one another. Men are dependent on other men for their education, their support, their nurturing, their protection, and their moral ideas.

An English guide at the Cathedral of Chartres outside Paris concludes his tour with a short discussion of the Great Judgment scene sculpted on the doors of the cathedral. "Why," he asks, "is it a 'last' judgment? Why are men not judged immediately upon their death?" When no one answers, he says, "Because men's influences for good or evil last far beyond their lifetimes. No final judgment is possible until the very end of time."

The simplistic idea of the victimless crime ignores the tangible influence of public morality on society. The idea is rightfully suffering attrition in our times. More people are coming to realize that ideas have consequences. A good example is the current debate on pornography. Pornography has long been the primary example of the consensual victimless crime. What a person reads in the privacy of his bedroom, the ACLU briefs state, is nobody's business but his own. Others have begun to understand, whether or not they credit statements made by Ted Bundy about the role of pornography in his descent to barbarous behavior, how much such sordid material affects the society outside the bedroom. There is a spillover effect of that material on others. In some cities, feminists have sought the passage of a law making the sale of pornography a violation of women's civil rights because it demeans women.

Common sense suggests a broadening of the concept of the victim. A visitor to San Francisco, trying to walk his child through streets filled with pornography, prostitutes, and transvestites, can no longer believe that these ideas have no impact on others, despite their consensual nature. A visitor to a vice squad's portrait gallery of prostitutes, each shown successively after a sequence of arrests, reveals the horrible price paid by the prostitute.

The law itself has never adopted the concept of a victimless crime. Some libertarians rally around slogans that suggest the law has no place intruding into the privacy of a person's bedroom. Like most slogans, it is better chanted than analyzed. In fact, the law always has had a discrete interest in private bedrooms:

What goes on in the bedroom: If what goes on in the bedroom has detrimental social consequences—incest, for example, or statutory rape—the state has a right to intervene, regardless of whether there was consent.

Who can use the bedroom with protection of marriage laws: The state is unashamed to set rules on who can get married and who can get divorced.

The consequences of bedroom activity: The law allows courts to inquire of acts inside bedrooms, after the fact, to determine the paternity of children, to enter private homes to determine custody and guardianship of children, and to set appropriate visitation rights conditional on fulfillment of requirements the court finds necessary.

The business bedroom: The criminal courts are

interested in what goes on in a brothel behind pulled curtains because it can affect individuals, community health, and families, and impose substantial social costs on society.

The number of wives in the bedroom: Few societies are willing to sanction polygamy, no matter how private and consensual. While courts have recognized a legitimate zone of privacy, they have never accepted the simplistic appeal to leave unanalyzed private, consensual sexual activity. They know better.

For the same reason, the law cannot ignore the influence of sodomy. The existence of a public homosexuality in our times has a powerful influence on the kind of society we have—the clothes we wear, the music we listen to, the preaching we hear from our pulpits, the treatment given our children, the lives lived by homosexuals themselves. We live, as philosopher Richard Weaver once said, in an increasingly effeminate culture. Homosexual author Dennis Altman has called the influence so great that it amounts to "the homosexualization of America."[1]

In analyzing whether homosexual conduct can be prohibited by ordinary statutes, therefore, it is important to consider whether homosexual influence in society is beneficial or detrimental. What is the influence of homosexuality?

Homosexuality's detrimental impact on society can no longer be disguised. Homosexual conduct injures others through spillover effects, the homosexuals themselves, the latent homosexuals recruited into overt conduct, and society at large.

INJURY TO OTHERS

The medical dangers of homosexuality have already been discussed (chapter 2). The evidence can no longer be ignored. Homosexuals threaten communities with hepatitis, exotic infections, and AIDS. The new findings on AIDS have destroyed the gay rights' slogan that so long as homosexuals don't injure anyone, what they do is their business. If promiscuous homosexuals are capable of causing death through sexual contact, their slogan becomes irrelevant. Homosexual acts pose a medical threat not only to homosexuals, but also to those who need blood and to innocent partners of bisexuals. One homosexual said that, although he had AIDS, he never told his frequent sex partners because he was afraid of losing his sexual opportunities.[2] AIDS also creates a substantial expense for the community. An assistant director of the San Francisco public health department claims the "average hospitalization of an AIDS patient runs four months and costs $80,000."[3] Homosexual acts are not "victimless crimes."

INJURY TO HOMOSEXUALS THEMSELVES

The damage to homosexuals goes far beyond their medical problems. Their conduct leads to devastating psychological consequences. Though homosexuals frequently point to the American Psychiatric Association's decision to drop the designation of homosexuality as a sexual deviation (an action we saw earlier that was accomplished through the coercive efforts of homosexual militants), most traditional psychoanalysts continue to believe that homosexuality is "a disorder of psychosexual development."[4] The unnatural character of the act and the staggering recent showings of promiscuity have convinced most of the traditionalists that homosexuality is not normal; as one of them characterized it, "homosexuals . . . present a definite personality maladjustment."[5] According to an influential psychiatrist:

The homosexual, no matter what his level of adaptation and function in other areas of life, is severely handicapped in the most vital area, namely that of his interpersonal relationships. The homosexual is not only afraid of women and lost to all meaningful relatedness to them as a group and individually, but he also harbors the deepest aggression against men.[6]

Finding that an "obvious failure of function [means] agony, sorrow, tragedy, fear, guilt of both an unconscious and conscious nature which pervades the homosexual's life," he concludes:

Those apostles of doom and defeat who would have homosexuality declared "natural and normal" disserve the very cause they claim to espouse. Few physicians and other specialists devoted to the principles of scientific rigor and professional integrity will yield to such propaganda. It is the homosexual who will be victimized by these false "friends." True, it is difficult to know that one is ill, but it is far worse to keep experiencing symptoms and yet be told by supposedly qualified people that "You're all right. There's nothing the matter with you. Relax and enjoy it. It's all society's fault."[7]

INJURY TO HOMOSEXUAL RECRUITS

Homosexuality is, like all forms of behavior, a continuum. It reaches from casual thoughts and impulses to temptations, from temptations to discrete acts, from acts to habits, from habits to an entrenched life-style. Psychologists historically have called homosexuality "latent" or "overt." Not everyone with homosexual tendencies acts out his behavior, just as not everyone with temptations to steal, steals. Unless the inclination comes together with the opportunity, such latent tendencies may never crystallize into behavior.

The social acceptance gay rights laws give to homosexual behavior creates a climate in which opportunities for homosexual behavior multiply. As the restraints of law and public morality dissolve and homosexuality becomes publicly celebrated as a valid life-style, it is logical to expect more people to explore it. More latent homosexuals will find opportunities for overt behavior, and with that overt behavior will go the undeniable consequences.

Many homosexuals talk about recruiting apparent straights into homosexual behavior.[8] This influence can savage the person ensnared, who in different times may never have been at risk in the first place.

INJURY TO SOCIETY

The young. The growing influence of pedophilia and its alarming dimensions have been noted recently in an FBI report,[9] which includes the following facts: One child sex ring in North Syracuse, New York, boasted over twenty thousand customers. A guide called "Where the Young Ones Are" listed 378 places in fifty-four cities in thirty-four states where a child could be found for sexual services. Seventy thousand copies of the guide were sold for five dollars each in just over thirteen months. Katherine Wilson, the "Kiddy Porn Queen" arrested in Los Angeles in 1982, had a mailing list of thirty thousand customers who sodomized children.

Child pornography sales exceed five hundred million dollars annually. The FBI claims pedophilia is a growing subculture because of the lobbying effect of groups who argue for "children's sexual rights." At the forefront of this battle are the homosexuals. And, like militant homosexuals generally, the homosexual pedophile is promiscuous. According to the director of the Sexual Behavior Clinic at the New York State Psychiatric Institution, the typical pedophile has molested sixty-eight children.[10]

Prostitution. Prostitution, like child abuse, is not the exclusive preserve of homosexuals. But while a minority of heterosexuals use prostitutes, or have used them on occasion, few older, active homosexuals can live without them. Many psychologists have pointed out the preoccupation of these homosexuals with youthful, lithe bodies.[11] Such a preoccupation is, to be sure, not foreign to heterosexuals either. But while the heterosexual couple grows older together, the homosexual seeks sex in the same young age group, even as he ages. When he begins to lose his attractiveness, he has no choice but to buy sex. That need has given rise to a subculture of prostitution by boys and young men in the inner city.[12]

Wherever any concentration of homosexuals exists, there exists of necessity young male prostitutes. Every time a cruising homosexual picks up another boy for exploitation, another victim is created. One leading homosexual magazine describes without condemnation the scene on a boulevard in Los Angeles known for underage prostitution:

> Seemingly undaunted . . . literally hundreds
> of hustlers flock to "S and M" boulevard
> every week. Sometimes the atmosphere is

tense with competition . . . but for the most part an air of camaraderie prevails, assisted by the widespread belief that however plentiful the supply of hustlers, the demand is almost always greater.[13]

Children of homosexuals. A prime part of the gay rights agenda is societal blessing on same-sex marriages. Laws are being proposed around the country to permit marriage for homosexual couples. The existence of a gay rights ordinance might well be interpreted by a court to bar discrimination against homosexuals in the marriage relationship. Such an effect, however, could have a serious and sexually disorienting effect on children.

How is a child to behave with two male or two female parents? How is he to respond to their relationship with each other and to their relationship with him? How is he to understand true femininity or true masculinity when his most significant role models are homosexual parents?

What about the child raised in a single-parent home by a homosexual? What happens to the child who is exposed to the homosexual lover (or lovers)? Role models do have an impact. Common sense suggests that problems exist for the child who has never observed a normal parental relationship.

Ideological influence. When homosexuals are attracted to artistic careers, their influence can be magnified. The artistic director of the famed Minneapolis Children's Theater recently pleaded guilty to criminal sexual conduct for repeated sexual acts with children over the past decade. His preferences were long known by people in the community but were widely tolerated because of his influential status. Later, seven other employees of the Children's

Theater, all in influential positions, were arrested for sex acts with children.

Through influential people in the media, in fashion, and in the arts, homosexuals project their antifamily, sensual, and unisex ideas onto society and seek to shape it.

SUMMARY

The fabric of society is damaged by a subgroup of citizens with serious psychological and medical problems who, because they cannot procreate, must recruit. The ideology associated with a compulsive desire for same-sex sodomy will inevitably shape the way homosexuals see the world, and others will be influenced by that world view. By enacting laws against such behavior in the form of antisodomy provisions, society protects parents and children from sodomites, protects potential and incipient homosexuals from themselves, and protects itself from extinction. Furthermore, it teaches all who will listen that sodomy is antithetical to a healthy life-style.

Chapter 5, Notes

1. Dennis Altman, *The Homosexualization of America* (Boston: Beacon Press, 1982).

2. R. Henig, "AIDS: A New Disease's Deadly Odyssey," *New York Times Magazine*, 6 February 1983, 28-44.

3. Norris, *There's Nothing Gay about Homosexuality* (pamphlet available through Good Neighbors, Box 73, Clovis, CA 93612).

4. N. Meredith, "The Gay Dilemma," *Psychology Today*, January 1984, 56.

5. S. Hadden, "Homosexuality: Its Questioned Classification," *Psychiatric Annals*, April 1976, 46.

6. Charles Socarides, "Homosexuality: Basic Concepts and Psychodynamics," *International Journal of Psychiatry* 10 (1972):119.

7. Ibid., 123.

8. See K. Jay and A. Young, *The Gay Report* (New York: Summit Books, 1979), 253ff.

9. "Law Enforcement Bulletin," Federal Bureau of Investigation, January 1984.

10. Ibid.

11. See Meredith, "Gay Dilemma," 58.

12. E. Rueda, *The Homosexual Network* (Greenwich, Conn.: Devin-Adair Publishers, 1982), 57.

13. Ibid., 58.

Conclusion

T he political proposals advanced by an increasingly aggressive group of homosexual activists, who demand full social acceptance of sexual deviance, will continue to raise some of the most interesting and critical public policy questions throughout the 1990s.

These issues merit serious discussion and rational analysis. Unfortunately, gay rights proposals have often received neither. The seriousness of the issues has not been matched by a seriousness of analysis. There has been a curious inversion: a high level of public policy interest; a low level of public policy debate.

Contrary to conventional homosexual assertions, the fault lies principally with the proponents of such measures. Those who have studied homosexual initiatives have observed a fourfold tactical plan:

1. *Avoid, whenever possible, serious public debate over gay rights measures.* Gay rights measures are often timed to surprise possible opponents. They are frequently introduced toward the end of a legislative session, and in haste. In states with no referendum

procedure, they are usually proposed in off years so legislators who vote for them need not fear a personal referendum that could lead to removal from office. Often, homosexuals seek to persuade governors or mayors to issue executive orders barring "discrimination" on the basis of "sexual orientation," effectively insulating the issue from the political process or from careful consideration by elected representatives. More recently, homosexuals have tried to repeal popular referendum provisions in city charters before seeking to pass gay rights laws, to avoid full-scale debate and democratic resolution of the issue.

These tactics are understandable, as a political matter, but hardly ideal if one desires sensible analysis and reasoned debate.

2. If public debate is imminent, seek to intimidate opposing voices into silence. The militant homosexual movement has not distinguished itself for tolerance to opposing views, or even good manners and common courtesy. The examples are plentiful.

- Adam Walinsky, a New York City public official and former adviser to Senator Robert Kennedy, opposes a gay rights measure in his city. His house is later set on fire.

- A major eastern college threatens Christian groups with loss of campus accreditation and expulsion for inviting a speaker to the campus to discuss the public policy ramifications of gay rights measures.

- Gay rights groups seek to impeach a student body president at the University of Minnesota for expressing an opinion supporting the U.S. Army position on homosexuality, a position frequently ratified by federal courts.

- A symposium is held in Southern California. Among the guests are a respected congressman and the chairman of the United States Civil Rights Commission. Homosexual activists threaten the hotel that has agreed to host the event. The hotel breaches its agreement and cancels the reservations. Another hotel is booked. Homosexuals visit the hotel in the early morning hours and set off stink bombs. The leader of the homosexuals publishes in the local newspaper a thinly veiled personal threat to the chairman of the Civil Rights Commission, suggesting that he bear in mind before coming to speak that the homosexuals know where he lives. They then later seek to invade the meeting and "shut it down."

- Prominent psychiatrists are shouted down as Nazis. A leading psychotherapist privately tells organizers of a symposium critical of gay rights that he agrees entirely with their position as a matter of public policy but is afraid to appear on a public panel.

- In Minneapolis, a member of the city council introduces a measure to control "cruising" for boy prostitutes in a downtown park. The park, long a haven for juvenile prostitution, has frequently had cars circling it nearly bumper to bumper at 2:00 in the morning. The council member, a woman, has long supported gay rights measures. But a group of "Friends Against Gay Suppression" (FAGS) storm her house, beat on the door with traffic pylons, and, when her husband comes out to plead with them to disperse, throw him to the ground.

These examples are a few of many, so many it is difficult not to see a pattern: intimidate the opposition into silence. The intolerance is almost entirely one way. Homosexual speakers are not generally shouted down, disinvited, or threatened. But those who do not share their views often remain silent for fear of loss of academic status, personal intimidation, or physical safety. Many voices that need to be heard are not.

3. *If debate occurs, use* ad hominem *arguments.* The homosexual activists like to characterize themselves as spokesmen for a rational, compassionate, and progressive enlightenment and their opponents as spokesmen for a superstitious, insensitive, regressive ignorance.

But when the debate is on, homosexual activists frequently resort to name-calling, while their opponents recite facts. Adam Walinsky may have admired Senator Kennedy on civil rights, but he is now a "bigot." Dr. Socarides may be a civil libertarian, but if he disagrees with homosexuals on whether their behavior is an illness, he is a bigot too. Any resistance to the homosexual agenda is a product of "homophobia" or "erotophobia."

The sophisticated name-calling may be good strategy in the modern battle of the sound bite, but it does little to advance public understanding of what is at stake.

4. *If the debate goes beyond* ad hominem *labeling, avoid at all costs discussion of homosexual behavior.* Homosexual strategy is simple: Keep the discussion as abstract as possible—civil rights, discrimination, minority status. Avoid being drawn into discussion of homosexual behavior. If someone brings up embarrassing facts about the homosexual life-style, accuse the person of being obsessed with sex and the merely physical dimension of human relationships.

The privileges sought for practitioners of homo-sexual behavior, of course, require a serious look at homosexual behavior. What *do* they do? What impact does what they do have on society? On themselves? But the conscious avoidance of such difficult (and unflattering) issues by proponents of gay rights invite policy makers to buy a pig in a poke—to extend social legitimacy to a life-style they only dimly understand.

This fourfold strategy is largely responsible for the perverse public policy twists and turns on this issue:

- We now know that anal sodomy is one of the most dangerous behaviors in America. It is the most efficient route of transmission for the most lethal epidemic of the century. It is associated with dozens of serious public health problems. Yet there are continuing efforts in state legislatures to remove prohibitions against it. The worse we know it to be, the less we want to prohibit it.

- The Department of Health and Human Services issued a report in August 1989 that detailed the enormous rates of suicide among adolescents who experiment with or engage in homosexual behavior. The findings are no surprise to those familiar with the effects of a homosexual life-style. Analysts both inside and outside the church have viewed homosexuality as a self-destructive life-style, yet where does the report place the blame for the phenomenon? If homosexual behavior is *the* variable associated with increased risk of suicide, would it be the behavior itself that is at fault? No, the report counsels. It is the fault of those who advance traditional morality, especially the churches. By calling "bad" something that is "good," they create a climate for teen suicide. If churches stopped teaching the biblical view that homosexuality is a self-destructive life-style, homosexuality would stop being a self-destructive life-style.

- Syphilis and AIDS have much in common. Both are sexually transmitted. Both are stigmatizing. Both are lethal, if they run their course. But syphilis is generally curable, and so it is even more important to stop the transmission of AIDS. Yet California had a law that made it illegal for a doctor (a) not to report a case of syphilis to the Commission of Health and (b) to report a case of AIDS to the same commissioner. He could go to jail if he reported the *more* serious public health problem, or if he did not report the *less* serious one.

These perverse results will continue to multiply as long as proponents of a homosexual agenda are allowed to play the game on their grounds. To win lasting victories, they must keep the focus of public attention on slogans and off facts. Gay rights proponents need to keep a high level of abstraction in the debate. Once the facts begin to emerge, the proponents retreat, like Bunyan's Giant Despair, at the first hint of daylight.

For that reason, those who oppose the abolition of moral norms and wish to promote the special place of the family in American life need to maximize the light shed on this issue.

Light illumines. Light is a natural metaphor for

intellectual discovery. Civil rights are important to any American, but their true basis and importance need to be illumined so citizens can be alert to distinguish between true and spurious claims to civil rights protection. Compassion is a Christian virtue, but that virtue needs to be illumined by balancing truths, so that the person who wants to be compassionate can know when that interest is best served by saying yes, and when by saying no.

Light exposes. Jesus talked of people who would not come to light because their deeds were evil. Light exposes the darkness and what is done there. Although there is a natural and wholesome reluctance on the part of decent people to explore the details of deviant behavior, that reluctance must be tempered by a need to give society a common-sense understanding about the nature and public costs of perverted sexual behavior. While the most egregious and detailed description of perverse acts is well left in darkness, society needs to know which kind of behavior it is being asked to accept as socially legitimate.

Light encourages. As darkness discourages, light encourages. Taking a stand on this issue necessarily requires courage. Those who oppose gay rights measures will often feel like a lightning rod, drawing down on themselves invective, insult, intimidation, indeed personal threats. To discourage opposition, the well-financed gay rights movement will continue to adopt the air of historical inevitability about their proposals. Proponents know that discouragement paralyzes the opposition.

In the face of this continuing assault, those who believe there are norms for sexual behavior and that "righteousness exalteth a nation" need both courage and good cheer. Because they walk in the light, they need not fear nor apologize for recognizing a difference between the normal and the deviant, the precious and the vile, in sexual expression.

Subject Index